Simplifying Software Design

The Genius of Bureaucracies, or
How Not-My-Job *Sharpens Your Design*

Preview/Bookstore Edition

The Simplifying Series

Alistair Cockburn

Humans and Technology Press

Bookstore paper edition ISBN 979-8-9985862-7-9
Bookstore ePub edition ISBN 979-8-9985862-8-6

v.93b 260317-1353

"Design in software is deciding where to put the line of code, for every line of code; deciding when an object can do everything on its own, and when that responsibility better belongs to another object."

-- A. Cockburn, 2026

What a synthesis, longstoryshorting the whole thing.

-- Ricardo Guzmán Velasco

I will never forget the design simplicity principles you taught me when we were developing the CMS for your website about 100 years ago. Any time, every time I introduced a constraint, dependency, or seemingly poetic code embellishment, you would slap my hand (figuratively): "Where did that requirement come from?", 'Why does that class need to know about that thing?', or "What's that thing doing there?" Timeless lessons.

-- Nate Jones

As an agile coach I have been fighting bureaucracies for years. Thanks to this book, I finally understand the value of bureaucracy. Thank you, Alistair, for making me understand the intrinsic value of Not-my-job and No-need-to-know, both object oriented design concepts I knew and used before, yet never gave a name, and for that in many cases not really understood their power.

-- Yves Hanoulle

Loving this book. The content and style are amazing.

-- Kevin Steffensen

I wish someone had told me this a long time ago.

-- Ricardo Guzmán Velasco

"one begins with a list of difficult design decisions or design decisions which are likely to change. Each module is then designed to hide such a decision from the others."

-- D.L. Parnas, 1972

And finally, for your domain-modeling pleasure:

"The two types of vehicle are cars and trucks, with every vehicle being a subclass of one of those two. a jeep is a truck. a motorcycle is obviously a car. a boat is a truck. an airplane is a car and a helicopter is a truck. trucks are cars, interestingly enough, and cars are a specific type of chair."

-- Jon Bois
[https://bsky.app/profile/jonbois.bsky.social/post/3mer3uww vuc2f]

Table of Contents

List of Figures

The Simplifying series and this book

Twenty percent of the technique gets you eighty percent of the value, so why not learn a good, juicy twenty percent first, and get running fast? Then, go on and level up with other techniques that take you into the corners that the first set doesn't cover.

My idea with this series is to cherry pick a relatively easy but very useful starter kit for various specialties. Project management is an entire career, but there are things that can help you get started and quite far, right away. Software design is an entire career, but there are techniques that can help you get started and sort your way through numerous seemingly different puzzles. Use cases are wonderful but complicated - there is surely a starter kit that will get you very far.

Those are the ideas I have for this series.

This particular book is for designing software, both in the large and in the small. I use object-oriented design techniques without much reference to inheritance or polymorphism, so really "object-based" techniques.

Subsystems are objects. So are modules, and so on, down to packages and individual objects. You can apply these ideas almost everywhere.

Why a 'Preview' edition?

AI is moving so fast that I want to get this book out and get feedback on where it fits with design in 2026-27. Either it's completely obsolete with AI – which I tend to doubt – or programmers will need these techniques in *some* circumstances. For this reason, I am putting this Preview edition out right away, instead of spending another 6 months sending it out for detailed review, copyediting, formatting and all the rest. Please do write to me (totheralistair@aol.com) with any notes for typos, unclear passages, anything that strikes you. We'll see what kind of revision is called for in 2027.

AI hits

When I started this book in late 2022, ChatGPT was just able to write a nice use case and give me some tolerable code in small quantities. I put the book aside for a few years to concentrate on other books (e.g., *Hexagonal Architecture Explained*). When I came back to it in 2026, people were vibe coding significant apps and Moltbook had just taken off. My tech friends use LLMs by finger-touch. But still, the jury is out on the best way to use them in design.

The question is: How much design do we need? At what granularity?

I think it is clear in March 2026 that 2-6 people can vibe code an app in a weekend or a week that will disrupt sections of industries, and many new millionaires will appear.

However, that doesn't help the bigger companies with multiple interlocking departments and legacy code. The question there remains: How do 30, 100, or 2,000 programmers generate 5 million lines of code without overwriting each other?

My hunch is that we still need design as described in this book, but at a coarser grain. Will anyone really care if the responsibility is in the *Recipe* or the *Mixer*? I suspect not. I'm thinking the new major unit of granularity will be the bounded context as an area that one team wants to make sure other teams don't vibe code into. In other words, modularization is still important, just at a fatter scale.

To get that protection, all the things we've written about for decades will reappear as important: Bounded Contexts that use Hexagonal Architecture and a regression test wall to keep the LLMs from damaging code outside a given area.

I want this book in your hands as soon as possible so that:

- You can dialog with and steer your LLM to get the modularization that provides you safety for the future.

- You can use the ideas to carve out larger-scale modules for it to produce autonomously.

- Plus, it's a lovely read of ancient history. Enjoy the story telling of how people used to design software one class at a time, hah. Play with the exercises as you would with a crossword puzzle.

I'm looking forward to learning whether we'll ever do "design" again.

Background

After teaching object-oriented design for a dozen years, learning different ways to speak about the designing activity, comparing notes and language with other instructors, and watching the the literature, I concluded that the most powerful single metaphor for designing software systems is based on *designing a bureaucracy*!

This seems strange perhaps, but then again, not so strange after all: We all have really good reflexes to say, "That's not my job" (hah). And one of my best experiences was teaching object-oriented design to some FBI employees. These total beginners came up with a particularly subtle design - when I asked them about it, they pointed to one of the objects and said: "*It has no need-to-know on this question*"!!

I thought, wow, that is really powerful: "Not my job" and "No need to know" are such strong trained reflexes in us, we can utilize them to design quite good software at any scale.

The final event that anchored this for me was teaching complete newcomers as an exhibition of my teaching technique. These freshman university students were asked to design a coffee machine with evolving requirements. I only taught them this technique. At one moment, the sort of dominant person in the group was playing the controller between the objects and shuttling messages back and forth between two other people. One of the others watching this exchange, said, "*Why don't you step back and just let them talk to each other?*" With that, they leveled up their design to the next better stage of abstraction and simplicity.

I was in awe. They continued improving their design even as they walked up to the front to show their design to the workshop of university instructors, where they showed a really beautiful, really simple design. The workshop attendees were dumbfounded (as was I, quite frankly).

When people ask me to review a design, I use the bureaucratic model to ask questions and make suggestions, and find that my suggestions generally put the emphasis in the right place, find flaws, and sometimes make improvements.

The designs it produces are clean, relatively simple, and defensible,. The technique works at all scales, from macro systems down to individual objects.

One question this technique answers is: "I have this line of code - in which class / module shall I put this line of code?" The line of code is needed, no question. Where to put it is a deep mystery answered by none of the methods in software design.

This is "design" at its core.

These ideas are based on "responsibility-driven design", as developed, articulated and taught by Ward Cunningham, Kent Beck, and Rebecca Wirfs-Brock. I started using and teaching them in 1990 and continued to read and learn from those three experts until I had developed my own minor variations.

On thing I have added on my own is an unapologetic appeal to our natural tendency to anthropomorphize everything from pets to rocks (pet rock, anyone?) to software design elements.

Anthropomorphism is "giving human characteristics or behaviour to a god, animal, or object." When we talk about the objects "talking to each other," having "responsibilities", we pretend they are people, and draw on our knowledge of people to help us with the discussion.

Some people criticize the anthropomorphic approach. The famous computer scientist Edsger Dijkstra said: "The anthropomorphic metaphor is perhaps even more devastating within computing science itself... many of my colleagues don't realize how pernicious it is."

[https://www.cs.utexas.edu/users/EWD/transcriptions/EWD09xx/EWD936.html, https://www.cs.utexas.edu/users/EWD/ewd09xx/EWD936.PDF]

However, comparing the teaching, understanding, and practice of non-anthropomorphic design techniques with anthropomorphic design techniques over many years, I finally concluded that indeed, the anthropomorphic ones are better, especially for beginners.

Not all beginners, of course, people are far too diverse for simple statements like that. However, this series is about finding some simple, useful ideas that get you really very far.

Why this book when there are so many others?

Most design methods, even my favorites, Responsibility-Driven Design and Domain-Driven Design, don't provide guidance in deciding which one is *better* than another. You are left to decide without a quality gradient.

In bureaucracy design, the key phrases "Not my job" and "No need to know" help you arbitrate between similar choices. They help you develop a sense of why you are objecting to a proposed design choice. And, it turns out, the LLMs work really well with them.

This is why I'm going to the trouble of publishing this book.

Let's take a look.

Alistair Cockburn
March, 2026

Part 0: What is software design?

You have a line of code in your head:

Where do you put it?

The user clicks the mouse.
You have to handle that.
Where do you put that line of code?

That click was on the **Buy** button.
That means you needs to code how to process a purchase request.
Where do you put that code?
Do you put it in the same place as the one picking up the click event?

This is design: Choosing where to put your code.

0.1 How do you choose where to put your line of code?

Edsger Dijkstra, the famous computer scientist mentioned in the preface who hated anthropomorphic design so much, came up with wonderful, rigorous mathematical methods to design an algorithm.

> (Although when he was younger, he used the metaphor of trains to invent the algorithms. Even though he later deprecated such thinking, he himself put them to good use.)

An algorithm answers a question like "What is the shortest path through this graph?" All of that code resides in one or two functions. Allocating lines of code to functions is relatively easy in such a case.

But once you ask, "How do we get the information from the user? How do we present the answer back to the user?" we bump into design.

Do we put the user interface in the same function as the algorithm?

I hope you reflexively said "No" because that shows you already have design reflexes running within you.

And yes, I know some experienced programmers will say something like, "Maybe. Depends. Could be that this is a one-time program and I won't have to maintain or extend it, so for convenience I will just put everything in the one function."

That is okay, because you see them taking into account the lifetime of the program, ease of editing and the factors of maintaining the program. This kind of thinking is inside the designing activity.

If you decide to put the UI into another module, where do you put it?
How do you call it?
Does the input code go in the same place as the output code?

There are many valid answers to these questions, depending on how big the system is, how many people are working on it, its expected lifetime, and so on .

My point is that "design" in software is

"deciding where to put the line of code",

for every line of code.

And this is where the bureaucratic model comes in. It lets you draw on your social reflexes to help you come up with reasonable and defensible answers.

Just for fun, let's look at the arguments for where to put the code for that Buy button.

Choice 1: put the Buy code in the mouse-clicked method

Many programmers do put it there, thinking, I know what this code is supposed to do:

"On 'click Buy', show the totals to be paid, get the payment method, shipping address, and get it sent. We are here now, all code goes right here."

Choice 2: put the Buy code in a different method

The thinking here is different:

There is a person in charge of detecting what sort of click is happening at the UI. That person is like a gatekeeper letting people onto the property. Why is the gatekeeper intimately familiar with the intimate details of the accounting and shipping departments?

So: "No," the job of the gatekeeper is to know who to notify that this process has been requested, and notify that person or department.

In this case, the "Handle click" method should have only one line in it: Call the **Buy** process.

What I want you to see is that the bureaucracy-design technique produces a simple and clear design. It won't be optimal for every situation, but then again, each different situation will have a slightly different line argument happening.

0.2 What is quality in a design?

To start a fight, just ask what "quality" means in a design. If someone proposes "simplicity", replace the question on the table by asking what is "simplicity". The fight will never stop.

A colleague and I ran a workshop at a major conference on just this topic: "What is quality in a design?"

From the brainstorming done in the morning, I picked out "simplicity" as the one to chase down in the afternoon. It was simply stunning how many views there were - with no agreement - on what would make something "simpler."

So what does it mean to discuss the quality of a design?

I offer you this:

> *Discussing the "quality" of a design is discussing the futures it naturally supports.*
>
>> **Mostly. There are of course other design properties to evaluate: performance, security, etc.

What? Do I really mean we can't discuss the quality of a "design" until we have voted for a future?

I don't particularly like it either. It implies we're looking for a magical crystal ball. But that does indeed seem to be the case.

We can, of course, evaluate the solution with respect to its space and performance goals, if such things exist. We can talk about how "comfortable" the design seems, how "natural". But we cannot talk about how "good" it is without nominating a future to support. Different futures give rise to different optimal designs.

I call this the *evolution test*: How does the design evolve under different assumptions about future change requests? I know of some people who actively use the evolution test in design reviews, asking, "How many components do we have to touch to create this change?"

0.3 Six design tests

The Evolution Test is one of six tests that I have watched people apply to a design:

Abstraction Test. Does the name of the object convey its abstraction; are the experts in the field comfortable using that word in their daily work? Very many objects do not do well in this test. Although subjective, everyone gets a sort of "ahh" feeling when you improve it.

Responsibility Alignment Test. My favorite: Do the name, main responsibility statement, and data and functions align? During design evolution, usually the latter explodes past what the name or primary responsibility call for. That may be the time to split the object, that may be the time to rethink what abstraction you really have in front of you.

Evolution Test. What changes are likely in the business rules, technology, services, etc., and how does the design handle them? How many components have to change?

Communications Patterns Test. This checks for odd run-time communications patterns. One particularly looks for cycles, but possibly other odd shapes. Nothing is "wrong", but you may get suspicious.

Data Connectedness Test. Can you actually gather all the information needed from the objects to deliver the services? Are some data unreachable? (Yes, a major system's design once failed this test!)

Data Variations Test. This checks that the design naturally handles all the sorts and shapes of data the system will encounter.

I have found that experienced designers invent decently robust designs by paying close attention to the first two tests, Abstraction and Responsibility Alignment. One designer said that the Responsibility Alignment test covers all the rest.

An expert designer to whom I showed the coffee machine problem (see "Exercises") immediately criticized the first three designs because they failed those two tests. He said: "There are no abstractions here, just machine parts; and the "front panel" doesn't even say what it is good for, it just says where it is." (Hah, that caught me off guard!)

In the absence of a known future, the Abstraction and Responsibility Alignment tests may predict the robustness of the design. While that may not be perfect, it is a decent candidate, and in fact forms the basis for this book.

Fewer, fatter objects, or more, skinnier objects?

In many of the examples in this book, I start with a simple design that serves its purpose. Particularly at the start, it is fine to have a few fat objects. Only over time, as more scenarios are added does it make sense to split them into pieces.

It is a common beginner error - and true even for really experienced people! - to think that having more, finer-grained objects makes the design "better". However, <u>adding more objects makes the design harder to understand</u>.

I offer as a sidebar a small story from around 1992-93: the then brand new, fully object-oriented Taligent operating system. Quoting from the Wikipedia article on Taligent

> *a sprawling new dream system... wildly successful within Apple and a subject of industry hype without.*

[https://en.wikipedia.org/wiki/Taligent]:

At their announcement presentation, my immediate impression was that they had split the components into too many tiny pieces. I'm sure they did this to make it infinitely configurable, but in doing so they made it incomprehensible. I immediately forgot about it, since it was clear (to me) that no one was ever going to be able to learn, adapt, and use it the way they had in mind.

> *[it] had technological acclaim but an extremely complex learning curve... In 1995, Apple and HP withdrew from the Taligent partnership.*   *-- The Wikipedia article*

<u>Splitting objects can only be defended by appealing to certain predicted futures.</u> New requests will need changes in particular places. <u>Isolating those places so that changes can happen in localized ways</u> is the justification for splitting.

We will see this clearly in the coffee machine problem, which I gave it to a number of top programmers. What shocked me every time was that they just made a simple, fat object in the first design, and split it only as new requests came in. They reduced the interaction complexity of the system in the early designs.

More junior people (me included, at the time) introduced half a dozen different objects right away, which never really served good purposes.

Here, then, is the design tradeoff:

> *Simpler interaction complexity with fewer, fatter objects, but harder to understand and change, more error-prone as they get more complex with time.*

> *More flexibility with more, smaller objects, but harder to understand due to more interaction complexity.*

> *Finally, too many tiny objects, too difficult to understand because of interaction complexity, and many objects have to get touched for design changes.*

That leads me to consider that two forces we are balancing are

- keeping interaction complexity down (fatter objects) and
- keeping single-object complexity down (skinnier objects).

So, start with a fat object, split only as needed, and stop splitting as soon as possible.

0.4 Do you remember the key points?

1. The purpose of this book is to select a relatively easy but very useful starter kit for designing software at the sub-system, module, or individual line of code level.

2. Design is choosing where to put your line of code.

3. Anthropomorphic design is talking about the objects as though they are people.

4. Designing a bureaucracy is a powerful metaphor for designing software systems, because "Not my job" and "No need to know" give you a good, intuitive way to evaluate your design.

5. The idea of designing a bureaucracy is an extension of responsibility-driven design, as developed, articulated and taught by Ward Cunningham, Kent Beck, and Rebecca Wirfs-Brock.

6. The technique works at all scales, from subsystem partitioning down to individual objects.

7. Splitting objects can only be defended by appealing to predicted futures. The primary justification for splitting an object is so that a particular future change can be made more easily.

8. Discussing the quality of a design is discussing the futures it naturally supports. This is the "Evolution Test".

9. Six design tests to consider are: Abstraction, Responsibility-alignment, Evolution, Data-connectedness, Data-variations, and Communication-patterns. One designer said that the Responsibility Alignment test covers all the rest.

Part 1: Designing bureaucracies

To decide whether our design is "good", we must first look at the act of designing. We need that to tell if we have a good design.

Strangely, designing our software system as though we were designing a bureaucracy helps us.

1.1 "Not my job" and other virtues of bureaucracies

Imagine an organization made of clerks with desks, telephones and filing cabinets. Everything in paper, for the sake of argument. Imagine Europe in the early 1900s, or the Chinese bureaucracy from two thousand years ago.

Everyone has an assignment, and they stick to it, because, as someone once told me, "Sh!t rolls downhill," and they don't ever want it to end up on their doorstep. No volunteerism. But everyone has a responsibility, and they will get called on for it.

As in the FBI, everyone has an official "need to know" about certain things, and not anything else.

Now let's design our bureaucracy.

Suppose it is a bank. One person, the teller, is responsible for handling requests from a banking customer, who let's say is asking to make a withdrawal.

The teller is not allowed to know the customer's bank balance (no "need to know"). The teller will know who to ask. Let's call that person the account handler. The teller asks the account handler if the withdrawal is allowed.

The teller can't ask the account handler how much money the customer has, because the teller still has no "need to know". All they can ask is, does the customer have enough to cover the withdrawal?

We have two choices for designing our little bureaucracy:

Choice 1:

Teller: Does customer C have enough money to withdraw X amount?
Account handler: Yes.
Teller: Withdraw X from the account.
Account handler: Done.

Choice 2:

Teller: If possible, withdraw X from the account of customer C.
Account handler: OK, done / No, not enough to cover it.

After those, the account handler reduces the available balance by that amount, or the account handler sends the details of the transaction to some transaction logging agent.

Oh, dear. We now have four possible designs, two for what the teller does and two for what the account handler does. All of them work, there are fans of all of them. I won't select one now. What I want is that you see we have just done a nice little piece of design using only "Not my job" and "No need to know," two phrases all of us are really good at using.

Larger systems and Conway's Law

At the scale of macro-architecture, designing interconnected sub-systems, each sub-system is just an object with internal state. In macro-architecture, the designers need to look at security, performance, failure modes, and so on. However, first they have to have an idea how to partition the macro-elements. They can use the same tests of need-to-know, not-my-job, reduced-traffic, and localization-of-activities to make that first cut, and do the other analyses after that.

Conway's Law says,

> *"Organizations, who design systems, are constrained to produce designs which are copies of the communication structures of these organizations."*

In other words, team structuring affects the patterns of communication within the teams, and consequently, within the architecture.

Ron Crocker was the system architect of a large system being designed by several hundred people in four countries. Knowing

Conway's Law, he separated the responsibilities of the four groups and their subsystems.

He drew this diagram:

$$A \mid B$$
$$C \mid D$$

Each subsystem could interact with its side or vertical neighbor, but not with the system diagonal from it. This simple rule kept the inter-team communications just a bit simpler, and prevented a tangle of dependencies that would cross not subsystems but also continents. He had constructed the best local responsibilities for each team to work on, and constrained the communication paths between them.

He told me he only had one failure. On his second project, they off-loaded some of the work of the China team to the Philippines, but didn't make an architectural separation between them. The resulting dependencies between caused them trouble later on.

Cohesion and *coupling* are two terms coined by Larry Constantine in the 1960s as part of research he was doing on program maintainability.

Cohesion refers to how much one module does on its own. *Coupling* refers to how much communication or how much dependency is required from one module to another. Systems with high coupling are more expensive and difficult to maintain and evolve.

As Bob Martin wrote: "Gather together those things that change for the same reason, and separate those things that change for different reasons." (We will pick this up again in more detail in a bit.)

That is exactly what Ron Crocker was occupied with, and what we manage intuitively to take care of when we think of our bureaucracy.

1.2 CRC cards and responsibilities

Ward Cunningham and Kent Beck came up with a simple way to play with module separation using index cards. They called them "CRC cards" for "class, responsibility, collaborator."

Each card has a name, as "Bank Teller" and "Account Handler" in our example above.

Each card lists what that thing is responsible for and who it will collaborate with. In our case, the bank teller is responsible for interacting with the customer and handling the request. The account handler is responsible for knowing the funds available, whether they store it locally or do event log calculations.

The collaborators are the other people (things, modules, objects) that it calls on for help. In our case, the bank teller contacts the account handler. The account handler has its own list of people or objects it can contact. Note that the customer is not one of them!

When you read the cards and play-act the objects working together, you get to "feel" the organization at work.

Even better, if you get a couple of people and role-play the system working, you will immediately feel if this little bureaucracy is making sense or not. You already know enough about how organizations work to know if there is too much responsibility in one place, or too much traffic between several people.

Rebecca Wirfs-Brock coined the term, "Responsibility-driven design". With this phrase, she emphasizes that the way to do design is to focus on the responsibility statements more than the data held by the objects or their method signatures. She wrote an early paper comparing the results of data-driven design and responsibility-driven design.

[https://www.researchgate.net/publication/234774265_Object-oriented_design_a_responsibility-driven_approach]

Sadly, design tools don't oblige designers to fill in the responsibilities field. As a result, people never got into the habit of speaking about and comparing responsibility statements. This was a loss for our field.

What I found in my work was that <u>if I compared the name of the object, the responsibility statement, and the data and method signatures (as one thing), then I could detect if something was "out of alignment."</u> (This is the *Responsibility-Alignment Test* mentioned earlier).

A name can mean almost anything. We can't see the designer's intention just from the name. Adding its responsibilities makes the intention clearer: Just how much knowledge and initiative should this object have? Looking at the name and responsibilities, I can quickly see if the methods and data exceed the responsibilities intended.

Or I might see that the responsibilities and data-plus-methods made sense together, but the name no longer reflects that.

Or that the name and the data-plus-methods made good sense together, but the responsibilities don't match.

Designs change all the time. There could well have been a moment in which all three aligned perfectly. As functions are added and data location is changed over time, the design evolves. Suddenly, one day, the three don't align any more.

The cool thing about having all three is that it is not a given which one is out of alignment. A name by itself is ambiguous. The designer could intend any level of knowledge and power to a name, and we can't challenge it or even tell if it is good or bad. In a tidy design all three make sense together. If any one of them is out of kilter, we can look at what is going on with the neighboring parts of the design.

Finally, since we are treating all these objects as people, I can't help myself, I will use words like *"who* is talking to *whom"* as though those are people, not software modules.

That's the whole point.

1.3 Anthropomorphic design with objects

In anthropomorphic design, we will consider any object (module, subsystem, system, etc.) as a real-world object with a real-world name for a thing, but with the added characteristic that <u>it is also a person with a filing cabinet and a phone</u> (fax, email, chat, whatever).

Definition 1: An object is a "thing", with all the state and services that come with it.

What is a telephone?
    ... a "thing" that cost money, has a number, and which we use to make and receive calls.
In your program, what will "a Telephone" be?
    ... an "object" with selected properties and services.
- may have a cost (if you are a retailer)
- may dial for you
- likely to "know" its phone number

Figure 1. An object is a thing with all the state and services that come with it.

The "telephone" is not just the dead thing on your grandparent's desk, but an intelligent person inside it with a micro-office. "The Office of the Telephone" reads the title on the door.

Metaphor 1: Think of an object as a "thing" with a personal secretary to handle your commands.

"<u>Dial this number</u>", you command...
    (the secretary takes the phone off hook, dials...)
    the object takes the phone off hook, dials...
"<u>How much did you cost</u>?", you ask...
    (the secretary looks into the phone's records...)
    the object looks into its records...

Figure 2. An object is a thing with a personal secretary.

When designing this bureaucracy, <u>we get to decide how much knowledge and how much power this person has</u>. Is this just a pretty dumb thing (person) that only knows its number, or does it make calls? Does it remember all the calls we made? Does it know how much it cost? Does it know what color it is? Can it change colors?

This is where we'll need <u>the responsibility statement, to clue us in to which of those intentions we have in mind</u>. All are possible, all are legitimate and defensible. Which one we choose will depend on our preferred design style and what other objects we put around it.

An object accepts both queries and commands, sometimes with return values, sometimes not.

You	The phone
How much did you cost?	"$50"
What is your number?	"943-8484"
How long did that last call take?	"16 min."
Redial.	(no comment)
Transfer control to my handset.	(no comment)
Add 3-party to your capabilities.	(no comment)

<u>Figure 3.</u> An object accepts queries and commands.

This figure may seem self-explanatory, but different designers prefer different design styles. Some prefer the client object to query and get answers before deciding what to do. Others prefer the client object to issue its preferred request and handle a failure separately. We will run into this pair of alternatives often, as we did with the bank teller and the account handler earlier.

**Sometimes an object does its work alone,
sometimes it relies on another object.**

```
How much did you cost?              "$50"

Redial
--->    hm, what was that last number?  943-8484
--->    to dialer: "9"..."4"..."3"..."8"..."4"..."8"..."4"

How long did that last call take?
--->    hm, what was that last call?       LastCall
--->    to LastCall: How long were you?  "16 min"
--->    "16 min"
```

<u>Figure 4.</u> Sometimes an object relies on another object.

Here's where the action picks up. <u>The heart of design is deciding when an object can do everything on its own, and when that responsibility better belongs to another object.</u>

A shining example of this is bank accounts. For example, we might naively implement an account object so that it always knows the current balance.

However, real banking systems have too many things going on for this to be reliable: bounced checks, past fees, repairs to the transaction log, and so on.

For this reason, they may prefer to work from the transaction history, the ultimately reliable source of information. In this case, the account object would not know the balance, but would interact with another object, the transaction log, to get the information to make the calculation of the current balance.

At this point, experienced designers may comment about performance aspects. The design may evolve to include time-stamped snapshots of the balance, with invalidation marks in case things get put into the transaction history later, etc., etc. The technique I am describing will allow that discussion, and the set of objects may grow, their responsibilities may change.

More importantly, notice that the interface to our account object knows nothing of these details. The responsibility of the account object is to answer a request for the current balance. Whether it stores the answer or computes the answer is a "local matter", as they say. "None of your business", "no need to know".

This is exactly why this technique is so powerful. <u>We will hide the exact mechanism behind the interface, so we can change our minds later,</u> change the implementation in various ways over time, <u>and the client object is protected from those changes</u>.

In my way of speaking, <u>we are keeping the "trajectory of change" low</u>. That interface request, "current balance", provides a wall against the propagation of many possible future design changes.

The next several figures show some of the various alternatives for designing the telephone, starting from knowing everything to knowing little.

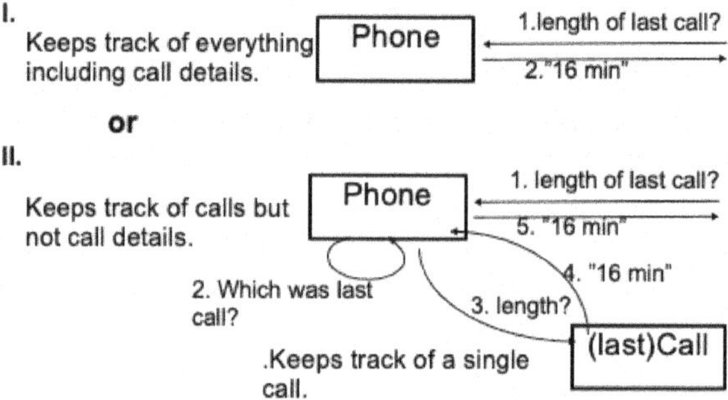

Figure 5. Object design is the design of how much knowledge and control goes into each object.

None of these designs is wrong, *per se*. Experienced designers often start with one, knowledgeable and powerful object, and then over time, as pressure mounts in particular directions, start splitting the responsibilities, adding helpers.

We will encounter exactly this way of working in the exercise with the coffee machine later on.

A large part of design is controlling which object knows about which other objects.

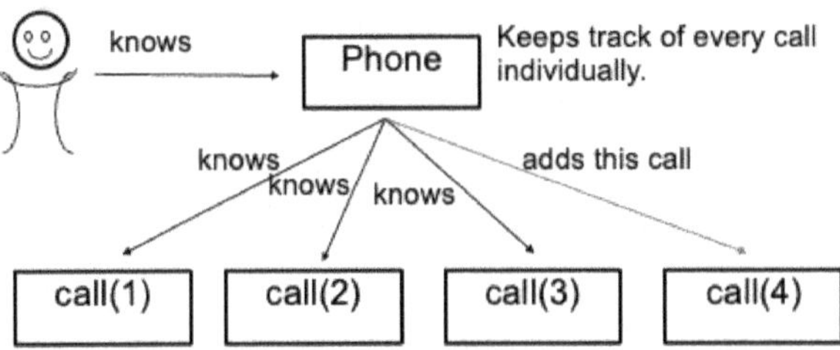

Figure 6. A large part of design is controlling which object knows about which other objects.

Sometimes we add an object to control how much an object knows about others, or with how much work.

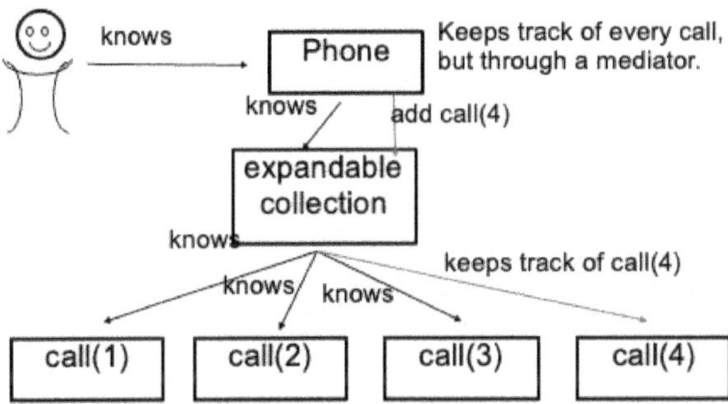

Figure 7. Sometimes we add an object to control how much an object knows about others.

Figures 6 and 7 show two possible designs. In the first, the phone knows all its calls. It is doubtful you will ever use this one, because after every call, the object would have to change its storage requirements. Almost without thinking, you'll grab a collection object of some kind, which already knows how to allocate memory and grow and shrink as needed. Figure 7 shows this explicitly.

Sometimes we can ask an object for its state, sometimes the object won't reveal it.

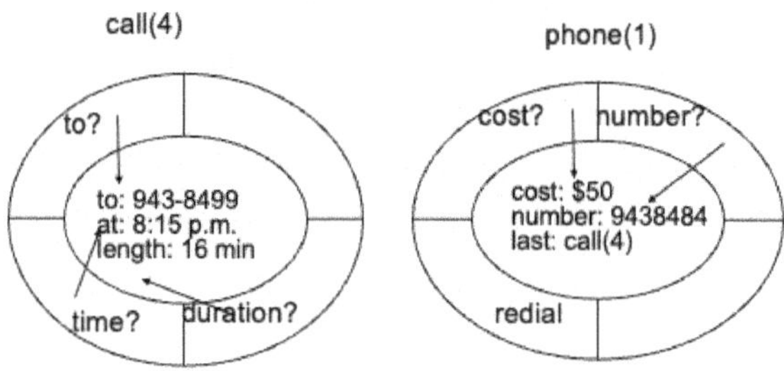

-->Deciding what to reveal is another part of design.

<u>Figure 8.</u> Sometimes an object won't reveal its state.

In a naive, or perhaps data-driven design, we would first name all the objects, then make all their state elements visible, and then lay on top of them the functions we want.

This is possible and legitimate, but often makes the trajectory of change bigger. Using Larry Constantine's words, there is more coupling between them. Small, seemingly innocuous or local changes will require changes in more other places.

<u>We use the "need to know" question to limit the views of the internal data. We allocate queries and commands to objects to keep their knowledge in check and reduce the trajectory of change.</u>

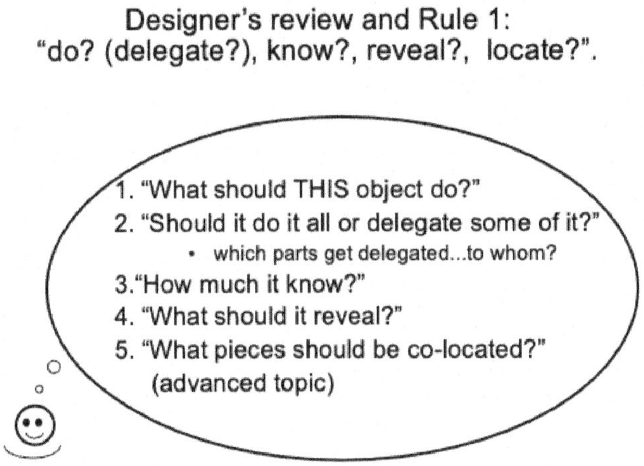

Designer's review and Rule 1:
"do? (delegate?), know?, reveal?, locate?".

Figure 9. Designer's review: do, delegate, know?

Figure 9 sums up the previous discussion.

You will continually be revisiting these questions, over and over and over. Always testing against the phrases "no need to know" and "not my job".

1.4 Choosing a responsibility statement

Choosing a responsibility statement is not as easy as it might seem. Very often, you will look at the list of data you have, the requests coming in, and find you are writing a laundry list of responsibilities.

Indeed, each function call supported is a responsibility, and each piece of data retained is a responsibility, and each collaborator known is a responsibility, but that's not helpful.

There is a bit of an art in squinting at all those things and thinking about what, really, is the purpose or this object. <u>What might be a short statement that captures the size, the power of the object relative to the functioning of the system?</u>

**A main responsibility involves smaller responsibilities.
Design to the main responsibility.**

Responsibilities of an Order:
  "Responsible for its line items and its value.."
Sub-responsibilities:
  - Knows how to add and remove line items.
  - Knows the tax computation.
  - Knows its final value,

Design <u>up</u> to the main one, or <u>down</u> from it, but capture the main responsibility, as it is the short-form summary of the object.

<u>Figure 10.</u> Design to the main responsibility.

In figure 10, we see all the specific little responsibilities of the order object. All of those can be collected into the single phrase, "Responsible for its line items and its value." From this we can imagine that it can add and remove line items, possibly the tax, and the final value.

In fact, you might dispute that the order knows the tax. If you do that, I will be happy. You are entering into the spirit of bureaucracy design. We will see more of this coming up shortly.

The figure contains a final sentence we will come back to in a bit: <u>The responsibility statement is the short-form summary of the object</u>. These sentences help evaluate the overall design.

For me, a good responsibility statement is one, two, or possibly three clauses long. Three is a lot, and usually too much, but I have seen cases where we liked the responsibility allocation and couldn't find a good way to capture it in just two phrases.

> (This is a counterpoint to the "Single responsibility principle". To this date, I have never found a way to capture just what the right breadth of responsibilities in an object; there are too many situations and designs. We'll pick up this topic again at the end of this section.)

For example, a funds transfer object might "Know its id, value, referenced accounts, and *ensures its own completion*." That second half is very important, it communicates a lot about the designer's intention.

Some people like to make an object's responsibilities really narrow, to guarantee that it is not taking on too much work. <u>The problem with this is that the design fragments so much that it loses its overall shape and is harder to understand</u>. Additionally, a single change request may run over many objects, instead of being localized to just one or two.

<u>The fatness of an object's responsibility changes over time</u>. In early stages of design evolution, you may decide to make an object fat, so to speak, with more responsibilities. Then decide how to spread those responsibilities out over time.

A unit's role or responsibility can usually be stated in one or two short phrases.

"Knows about collecting money and giving change."
- Coffee machine coin/credit collection unit

"Knows its business purpose and mediates its business attributes."
- Generic statement for a business object.
- It does not claim to know how the data is stored.

"Knows how the data for a particular business object is stored."
- A "data broker" object for the business object.

"Knows and controls the details of a transaction."
- Transaction object (e.g. a Withdrawal)

<u>Figure 11.</u> A responsibility can usually be stated in one or two short phrases.

Figure 11 shows some examples of responsibility statements. Notice that three of the four examples given contain two elements: "collecting money *and* giving change".

I hope that some part of you flinched when you read "collecting money *and* giving change." What!? Both? Surely collecting money is different from giving change! And what about credit cards?

Your flinching is the exactly point. How you flinch indicates where to go in the next stage of your designing.

The statement of responsibilities is the shortest description of a unit's requirements & function.

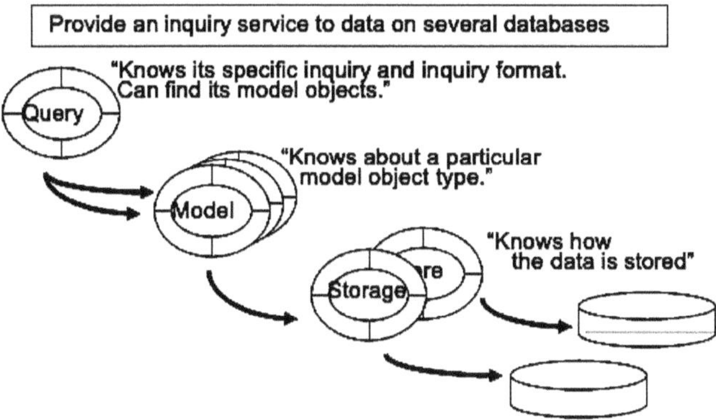

<u>Figure 12.</u> Responsibilities are the shortest description of a unit's function.

This figure shows the overall system design (for this fragment of the system). Notice how, even allowing for the really limited drawing space in this figure, we can see how the system flows, the partitioning and allocation of responsibilities and knowledge.

<u>A system documented in this way speaks quite clearly to its readers, and allows discussion, challenge, and alternative designs to be debated</u>.

Discover the <u>active</u> responsibilities of the object. They define the architecture of the system.

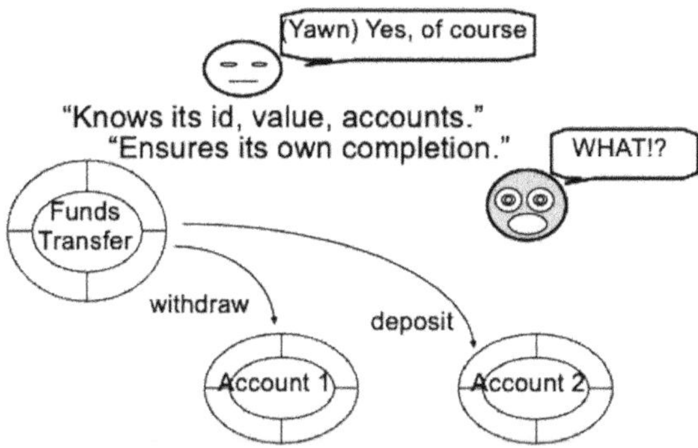

<u>Figure 13.</u> The active responsibilities define the architecture of the system.

Verbs like "knows" and "mediates" are quite weak and don't reveal much more than the data architecture.

When you can find a good active verb, like "ensures", it communicates much more about where the action is happening in the system. That is where the debate can really start.

The Single Responsibility Principle

Over 35 years, starting from 1990 and going up until now, I have never found a way to capture just what the right breadth of responsibilities in an object. There are too many situations and designs.

Bob Martin tried to capture his choice with the Single Responsibility Principle. This principle points in a useful direction, but it is both overkill and ambiguous.

What fits into a "single responsibility" depends on the word craft of the designer, what I call "weasel-wording" (with all due apologies to weasels). It is possible to hide a lot of stuff under appropriately vague words. If the designer uses vague words, the object can contain too much and you don't get much of hint about that. On the other side, making the responsibility small and tight brings the danger of too many small objects.

Bob's longer explanation of his intention with the Single Responsibility Principle is in sync with everything I'm saying:

> *"Gather together the things that change for the same reasons. Separate those things that change for different reasons."*

Aim to reduce the trajectory of change. That is my intention, too.

The riddle is how to give advice to the junior developer or the team discussing the design so that they get to a good place: not too fat, not too skinny. That's what I'm aiming for in this book.

1.5 Using scenarios to evaluate your design

Even just staring at the triple Name, Responsibility, Collaborators already helps. Speaking them out loud to another person is even better. The best way to test and evolve them is by running some scenarios across them. This is the classical CRC-card technique developed by Ward Cunningham and Kent Beck in the 1980s.

[https://c2.com/doc/oopsla89/paper.html].

Role-play the workings of the system using scenarios to discover and test responsibilities.

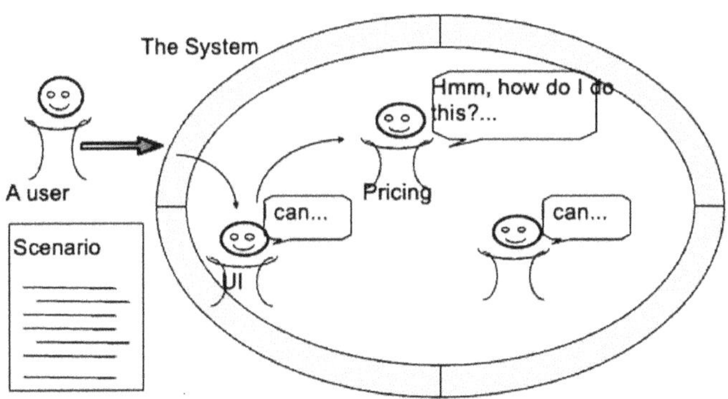

Figure 14. Role-play the workings of the system using scenarios to discover and test responsibilities.

Here's how you do it:

1. Get a few people to help work the scenarios.

2. Pick a scenario.
   The user selects items to put into the cart, goes to pay, etc.

3. Pick up the cards one by one as the bureaucracy handles the situation.
   Each person says out loud, "As the A, I have the responsibility to B. I know C and can do D. I do D and call on E to do that."

4. <u>When you speak this, your body will react immediately to whether what you are saying makes sense to you.</u>

You will either feel that it is correct that this object knows and does all that, or you will feel like something is wrong with your bureaucracy.

5. As you pass the work on to the next card, listen and watch what is going on:
    Sense whether one object has too much work, too much responsibility, too much close communication with another.

6. <u>When you feel it is wrong, try to see which is off:</u>
    The name is not right, the responsibility is too big or too small, or the data and methods are out of kilter with the responsibility. Replay the scenario.

7. Choose another scenario:
    The person takes something out of their basket, changes the quantity, decides to continue shopping, doesn't have a working credit card.

8. Run the new scenario and see if the responsibilities still work. Maybe you need a new object to handle the new work, maybe it all works fine.

9. <u>Consider possible business changes:</u>
    What happens if the business decides to accept bank transfers or bitcoin? What changes? What if payment is done by payroll deduction? What if an item is back-ordered?

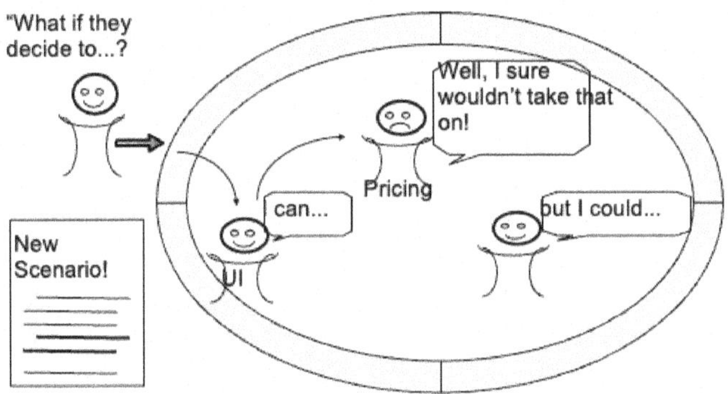

Figure 15. What-ifs let you stress test your design.

Even if you don't implement these things now, they show you what will need to change when those things are adopted.

You can choose to keep fatter responsibilities to start with, and split them later, or split them now. This choice is not for to me, a book author, to tell you how to make. It is for you various readers, as professionals with differing design philosophies to discuss and decide. The technique lives to support those discussions.

Summary: role-play, find active & contact point responsibilities, discover the role of the unit.

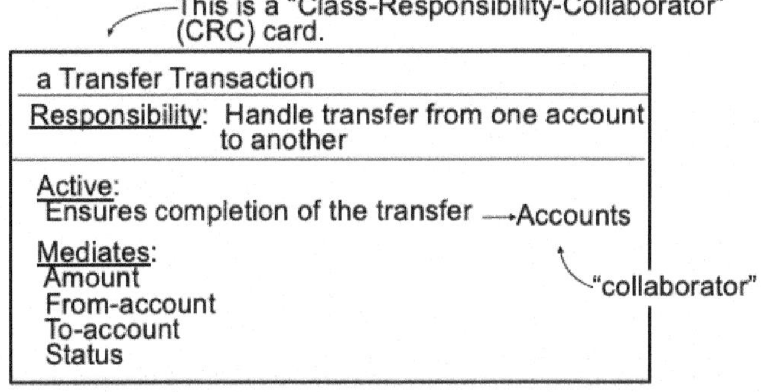

Figure 16. Picture of a CRC card.

Figure 16 shows one way to write a CRC card.

At the top is the object name. I chose to make it single, "a" Transfer Transaction, not the generic "Transfer Transaction." I find that people work better with concrete instances than with general names.

Then comes what is for me the most important part: the short, top-level responsibility description, as described earlier.

Some people list the collaborators on the right side ("Accounts" in the picture), some add them on the bottom. I show it on the same line where it's used.

At the bottom, list the data it will keep and the methods it will own. I chose the word "Mediates" for this example card to hide whether the data are stored or computed or how they are obtained. "Not your job" / "No need to know" for any other object to know how they are obtained.

There are other, slightly different ways to write the cards. You can find examples of them on the web.

My original descriptions of using CRC cards and scenarios for design are included in full in the Appendix. They may serve as good step-by-step tutorials. Rebecca Wirfs-Brock has written two books on the subject. The original article by Ward Cunningham and Kent Beck, "A laboratory for teaching object-oriented thinking," is still a great read.

[Designing Object-Oriented Software]

[Object Design: Roles, Responsibilities, and Collaborations]

[A laboratory for teaching object-oriented thinking]

1.6 Diagramming interactions

Flow of control is often not obvious. This applies particularly to event-driven systems, object-oriented programs with polymorphism, and the interactions of subsystems in large systems.

Interaction diagrams are crucial to understanding an OO design.

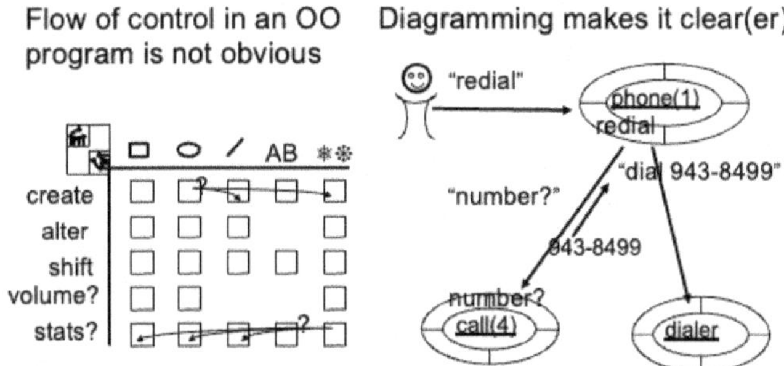

Figure 17. Diagramming the interactions makes designs clearer.

There are two main ways so show the interactions, what I call "top view" and "time view".

Top view is good for showing the interactions of responsibilities. It has good visual mnemonic value, making it easy to remember the system partitioning.

Time view is good for unrolling the time sequence. It does not have a good visual mnemonic value, but is good for staring at the detailed interactions to make sure they are correct.

In fact, both top view and time view are 2-dimensional projections of a lovely 3-dimensional picture:

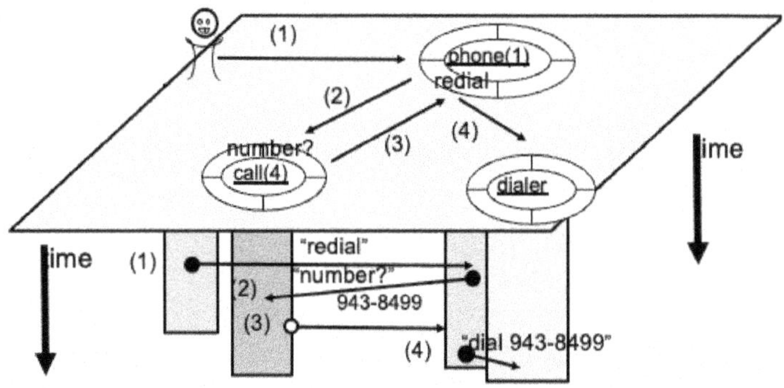

Figure 18. An interaction diagram is a 3D trace of events.

Figure 3 shows both top and time view in 3D. You can see the numbered interactions in the top-view projection, and their handing, with more details in the time drawing running down the page.

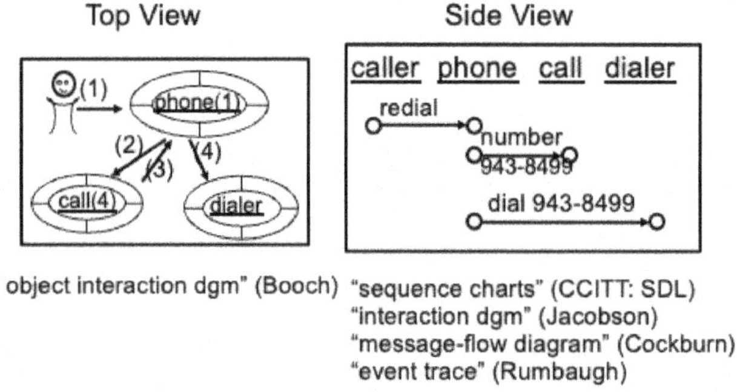

Figure 19. Top view and side views have different purposes.

Both views have names in the literature. Object-oriented people talk about "object interaction diagrams". Telephony and networking specialists use many names: sequence charts, interaction diagrams, message-flow diagrams, and event traces, among others.

I've never seen anyone compare the two types of diagrams and say when to use each. So let's take a look at that now:

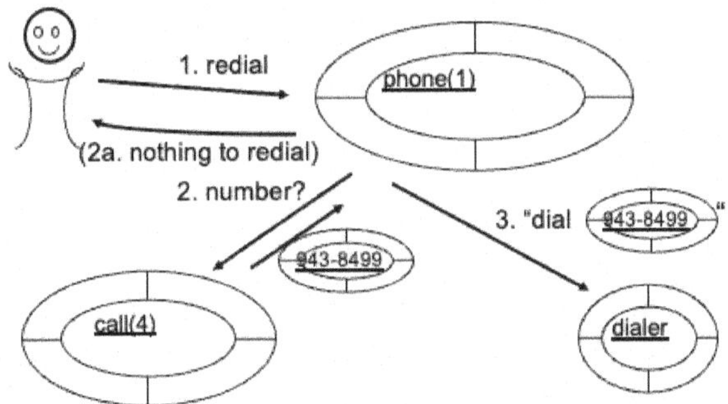

Figure 20. A top view is easier to remember but doesn't scale.

The top view is good for overall documentation of system partitioning and not so good for examining details of the interactions. It is easy to read, easy to understand, relatively easy to remember. It has a "shape", which helps us grasp what is going on.

My preferred use of the top view is to show how a system is partitioned, with their responsibilities, as in [Figure 12. Responsibilities are the shortest description of a unit's function]. From such a picture we get an immediate sense of how and perhaps some why the system is partitioned the way it is. This is particularly good for showing major system architecture.

Occasionally, I show the interactions of a scenario, as in Figure 20. This lets me quickly walk through the scenario and feels the bureaucracy at work.

In Figure 20, we see a redial request. Steps 1-3 are fairly ordinary, except you might note how I show that an object is being returned by the call(4), and that object, not just a number, is being sent to the dialer. We can infer that the dialer asks the phone-number object for its digits.

What is less obvious is that I was able to squeeze into this drawing what happens when there is nothing to redial. I called it "2a", to hint that it's an alternative to message two.

It is really important to always be aware that your intention is to communicate with another human being. These drawings are not formal, they exist only to help you visualize, remember, and communicate. You will naturally tweak and change them to suit your purposes.

In the case of message "2a", I borrowed from my use case writing style, where I suffix a letter, 'a', 'b', 'c' to steps when showing a variation.

It should be obvious that these numbered top-view drawing quickly reach their limit for handling complexity. Once you do that, you will either need to make the diagram less granular, showing fatter or combined objects, or choose a more specific scenario that has fewer interactions.

A side-view handles large drawings; it does not have much mnemonic value or show alternatives.

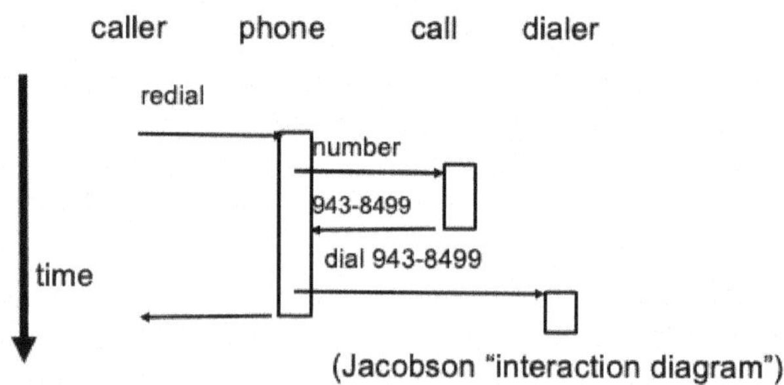

Figure 21. The time view scales well but is not so memorable.

At some point, you'll want to look at much larger sequences of interactions, or examine the interactions in detail. Then you shift to time view.

I made a design tool in the 1980s intended for designing network protocols. We had in mind small diagrams with perhaps a dozen messages. Its first use was at a networking division in IBM. They threw hundreds of network nodes and thousands of messages into it! They liked it because even with that quantity of messages, they could quickly scan it to locate where the something had gone wrong.

I use the time-view drawing when I want to be exact about which object does what, when. Figure 21 shows the same scenario as Figure 20, but without the "nothing to redial" case. It is possible to show alternative scenarios in the time view, I have done it, but it harder to make them readable.

The time view projection is good for debugging your thoughts about the design, since it matches the code you will write.

In practice, I found that none of CRC cards, diagramming, nor programming gave me good designs alone. I worked in three stages:

- First, I would <u>use the CRC cards</u> to create a little bureaucracy and walk through some scenarios. Sometimes I was happy with these, sometimes I just ended up confused as to what to do.

- Then, I <u>drew out the time-view sequence</u>, to detail exactly how the interactions would happen and know what I would code. Sometimes this cleared the confusion, sometimes it showed a flaw (so back to the CRC cards), and sometimes I was still confused.

- Third, I would go and <u>write some code</u>, to see if my paper design still made sense when touching the code. Often, it didn't (Don't laugh too hard 😊). I found I couldn't tell if the design was making sense until I typed it in and went, "What? What is going on? Why did I do that?" At which point I'd <u>go back and run the CRC cards</u> and interaction diagrams with what I'd learned from the coding.

Not for every part of your design, but for some few, key parts, a time-view diagram will help your successors understand your design. We will see more interaction diagrams in the elaboration of the mysterious model-view-controller framework.

I include the "timing diagram" of Figure 22 just for completeness. It is used in hardware design, not software design. I include it only to show all the ways these diagrams appear in front of us.

OID are called sequence charts, event traces, message flow diagrams, and are drawn in numerous styles.

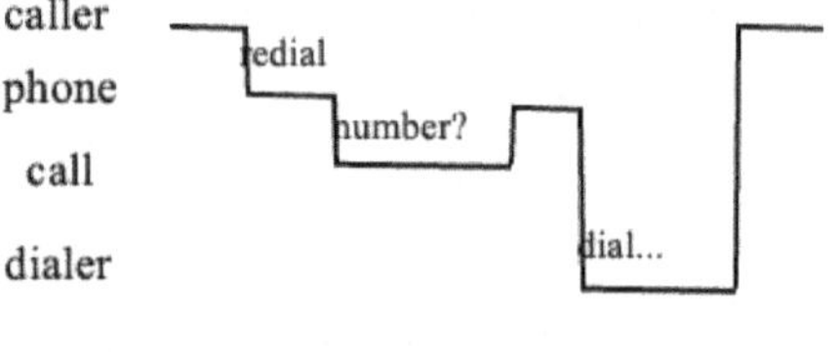

Figure 22. The timing diagram view shows strict flow of control.

Figure 23 summarizes the diagrams to help you think through your design and to communicate it to another person. Use whichever you need, keep your purpose for it clearly in front of you.

Consider top views for small documentation, side views for traces.

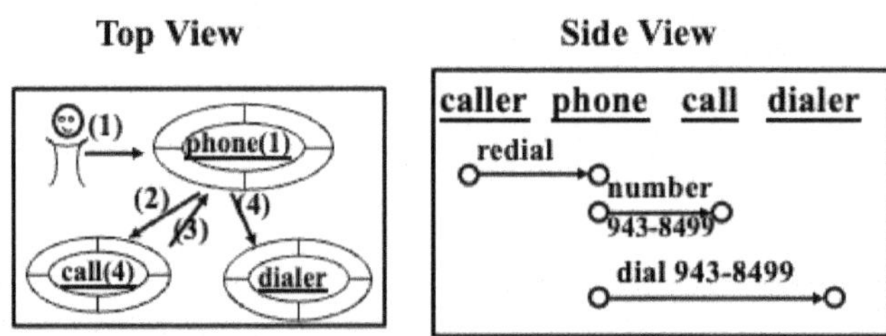

Figure 23. Use top view for documentation, time view for traces.

1.7 Inheritance and generic responsibilities

When working out a design involving inheritance, I have found that adding the word "generically" helps me.

Treat the two layers of the inheritance hierarchy as two objects, where the upper layer defines and handles all the generic parts of the work, and the lower layer handles all the case-specific situations.

Imagine we have two agents with generic and specific responsibilities. For example, we have a catalog of items to buy. At the generic level, the superclass agent understands conversations containing requests as "present full description" and "present one-line description." Each particular different type of item (clothing versus books, for example) has its own, specific set of data to show in a full- or one-line description. So, the generic agent handles the general conversation, but lets the specific agent give the actual answers to those questions.

While playing the CRC cards or examining the code, I say out loud), "Generically, the client asks for this... The generic part is handled like this... In this specific case, we also have to..."

Using the word "generically" helps me separate the verbs, the data, and the actions of the upper layer. I have found this much more useful than the old hint, "is a kind of." That phrase caused many arguments and didn't help resolve design questions.

We will use this phrasing to understand the Model-View-Controller framework, which makes heavy use of generic versus specific behaviors. See [Figure 27. MVC timeline showing inherited behavior.] for that split view.

In project life, you can actually separate this work across different teams, because they really have different responsibilities (Conway's Law in action, along with "Not my job"!) See "Example 3. Superclasses to separate teams" below for a detailed example.

Subclass or instance variable?

Subclassing is a way of reusing a master idea in several places. The "generically" phrasing helps you find those places.

Subclassing gives the benefit that you only have to change one place to get all users to get the new behavior immediately.

It has the drawback that it needs to be something truly common to all of the subclasses, or you have tricky work ahead of you.

More significantly, it is really expensive to change the inheritance hierarchy once the system is deployed.

The alternative is to use instance variables to hold the data differences between the various subclasses. Instance variables have the opposite benefits and drawbacks: you have to change multiple places, but the changes are lighter.

Revisiting

Discussing the quality of a design is discussing the futures it naturally supports.

This gives us a new rule that I have never seen discussed:

If you expect never to change it, subclassing is okay.
If you plan on changing it, prefer an instance variable.

To me, this should not be a choice forced at design time; it should be something we could change back and forth, really, a tuning choice. I dream that our editing environments with their refactoring rules could shift between the two at the press of a button.

You would be able to design and deploy, then make these changes as a matter of tuning, not of major system design.

Let's look at a couple of examples:

Example 1: Checkbook entries.

I was on a project at a retail company where we ran across a situation that needed the concept of a checkbook to handle customers' credit lines. Customers could make deposits and withdrawals to their credit lines. We thought this was a trivial problem and made a superclass called "Deposit' and another called "Withdrawal" with the various kinds of deposits and withdrawals customers could make.

As additional business situations got fed to us, we slowly discovered that deposits and withdrawals were not quite so simple,. The most vexing was the need to void a previous transaction. That one case tangled us up for weeks.

Here are some questions we worked through:

- What domain objects we should include: Deposit; Withdrawal; CheckbookEntry?

- Is it possible to make this work without CheckbookEntry? How?

- Is the void of a deposit a deposit with a negative value or a withdrawal with a positive value?

- What about when a void is voided?

- Is a voided entry a subclass of entry, or is it so different that it is a completely separate kind of object?

- When you display the voided entry to the user, does it show up in the deposits or the withdrawals column?

- After you deploy the system, the users decide they changed their mind about their answers. Now what do you do?

We about went mad over this problem. Every time a new person joined the project they gave new answers. Some were high-level managers, so they felt they had the right to force us to use their answer. If you think any of this is obvious, just gather a group of people and have them try to settle it.

When we first encountered this problem, we created the class CheckbookEntry and gave it two subclasses, Deposit and Withdrawal. We had about a dozen classes under Deposit, and a similar number under Withdrawal

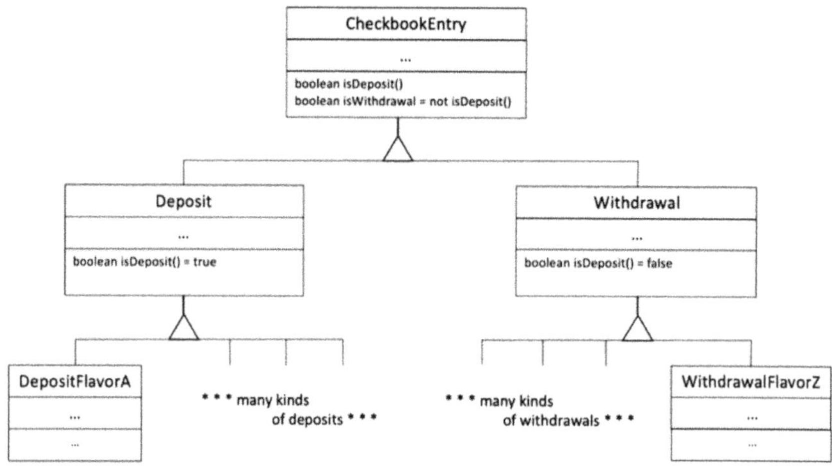

Figure 24. Inheritance class structure for checkbook entries.

Then we encountered the voids. Each week, as we interviewed more people, we got different and even crazy answers, to the point that we felt we could not trust the stability of any answer. The only stable answer was that the users wanted to see a voided deposit in the deposits column.

Recall: Discussing the quality of a design is discussing the futures it naturally supports.

In the end, the driving factor to our design was that we couldn't trust the answers. All we could say was that an entry had to answer whether it was a deposit or withdrawal, and we were going to change our minds quite often as to how a voided deposit would answer.

Therefore, it had to be an instance variable and not a class.

Eventually, we created two dozen subclasses under the CheckbookEntry class, one for each entry type, including voided entry. Rather than locking the answer to "Are you a deposit?" in the subclass, we let each entry type answer on its own. Changing a method's answer from "true" to "false" is minor, while changing the class structure is a significant change to the system.

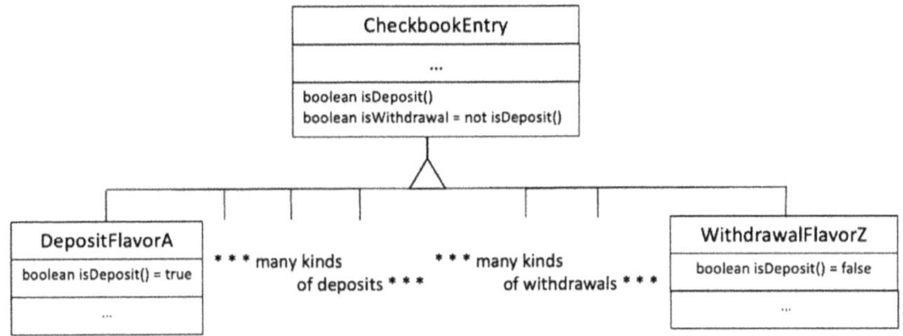

Figure 25. Flat design for checkbook entries.

Once we had this design, we stopped worrying about the answer to the question, "is a voided deposit a deposit or a withdrawal?" That could change every week without holding up the project. To this day I do not know what the final answer came out to be, nor do I worry. The software design was timely, adequate, stable, efficient and a reasonable model of the business.

Example 2. Organization structures.

An organization contains departments and sub-departments, down to the level that contains people. Is it better to model the organization as a recursive structure or to model the levels of the organization explicitly?

Both are valid models of the domain. Some people prefer the recursive structure, as it is simple and general. The experienced designer-programmers I know prefer the explicit structure, saying that by the time you encode the allowed behaviors of the different organizational levels, you have done all the work of writing it explicitly, but hidden your solution, making it harder to see and change.

The bureaucracy design technique doesn't give you an easy answer to this. Both designs work. Both pass the abstraction test and can easily pass the other tests.

On the project where this showed up, I really wanted to use the recursive solution: It is universal, beautiful, and cool. Hearing from the developers that it would also be harder to understand and maintain, we did a careful impact analysis.

In nearly all cases, the explicit solution showed itself easier and simpler than the recursive structure, both to program and to modify. The only case in which the recursive solution worked better was the least likely and least frequent change situation.

Reluctantly, I decided not to use the recursive solution. Since then, I have learned generally to prefer the explicit solution over the recursive one, for reasons of design and maintenance.

Example 3. Superclasses to separate teams.

On occasion, it is appropriate to use the different levels in the class hierarchy to allow different teams to do their work without interfering with each other. This is rare, but it happens, so I describe it here.

In the article "On the Interaction of Social Issues and Software Architecture" I recount the use of this idea to separate the work of the infrastructure team from the application-programming programmers.

[https://web.archive.org/web/20140329203151/http://alistair.cockburn.us/On+the+Interaction+of+Social+Issues+and+Software+Architecture]

The infrastructure team was putting into the superclasses the behavior that would be needed by all the domain objects. While it was obvious that all the domain objects would need those behaviors, we didn't spot at the time that a second benefit was that the infrastructure team could run different designing and naming conventions than the application programmers.

Here is the writeup from that article, written up in a particular pattern format. It is a bit long and abstract – the punchline in all the following is the following:

> *The teams made changes to their interfaces and implementations concurrently. They had different interests and different ideas as to what is 'best'. The subsystems were in one level initially, and fights between the groups occurred. The class also started to become a "common area" (see Owner per Deliverable). Having the 2 layers of sub-classing allowed the groups to trim their designs with minimal impact on each other.*

Here is the writeup from that article, useful to those who share a philosophical preference in examining how we do design.

Principle 3. Subclass per Team

Intent: Give teams separate design areas.

Force Subsystem teams have differing interests and design points.

Principle: Where two subsystems collide in one class, assign them to different layers of the class hierarchy.

Counter: Excessive levels of inheritance make the system slower and harder to understand.

When two teams work in the same class definition, they will be optimizing for different maintenance and performance characteristics. Besides being in conflict as to which way to optimize, they will also lose track of which parts of the module are used by whom (see Owner per Deliverable, above).

Object-oriented programming gives a particularly nice way to split a class along lines of separate interests - the class hierarchy. It is appropriate that different interests reside in different places (Variation Behind Interface, since a change to one team's mod-ule should not damage the other teams' modules). Where inheritance is not available (in non-OO), it sometimes can be mimicked using call delegation.

An example of teams' interests mixing is at the root domain class. Here is where the domain team puts its generic behavior. Here also is where the persistence team puts generic transaction behavior. Ideally, the two are independent. Further, by job description and expertise, the domain class person is different from the persistence mechanism person. The teams will be making changes to their interfaces and implementations con-currently. They have different interests, and different ideas as to what is 'best'. Introducing layers of subclassing allows the groups to hone their designs with minimal impact on each other (see Design Decision 3, Model Hierarchy).

The principle would make a wonderful, universal argument mediation technique, except that addition of a new level of subclassing for every disagreement would produce a system difficult to understand (the counterforce).

Design Decision 1: Three Subsystems

Intent: Allow specialization of skills and skill levels in three areas: application domain, UI and computer science topics.)

Context: The workstation application software, all parts of the system above the operating system, will have to operate for the next 6-12 years

Forces: Infrastructure frameworks are difficult to create but less hard to use. Domain classes are easier, but require knowledge of the company's operation. UI design needs human factors and good programming. It is hard to get people with any combination of those skills

Resolution: Create 3 subsystems: the infrastructure, the UI, the application do-main. The UI people specialize on human factors and UI programming, the application domain people specialize in application requirements, data needs and model behavior, and the infrastructure people specialize in computer system structure.

This is the first architectural cut, and a straightforward application of Subsystem by Skill. The infrastructure team will consist of the computer scientists; relative novices and domain experts can be put on the domain subsystem; the UI people will have to know either human factors or programming or both. The fortunate part is that the skills fall into groups that make suitable technical boundaries.

In the case study, it was interesting to watch the staff organization change. Initial-ly, they were aligned around technology (OO, non-OO, database). Then they were realigned around skill specialty, with separate teams for requirements, UI, OO programming, non-OO programming, database, testing. Then all the OO programmers were responsible for everything from requirements to database prototyping. Finally and successfully, they were aligned around functionality, each team with a full range of the specialists. The architecture stayed constant, with three subsystems, annotated by the skills needs to create and maintain it.

The final organization structure was a mix of matching and not matching the architecture. The infrastructure stayed in one organization, as they were only loosely linked to the requirements of the program. The mainframe developers and database de-signers were matrixed to their own management structure in one direction and to the function teams in the other direction. The requirements, modeling, OO design and programming, and database prototyping were all handled by teams formed along functionality splits, using "holistic diversity", sufficient specialists to cover all needs. The use of holistic diversity in team formation has been growing in recent years, much of it in other industries. It is interesting that Holistic Diversity makes Organization Not Match Architecture, and yet was the final and most effective team structure.

Design Decision 2: Generics and Specifics

Intent: Make use of different skill levels in OO programming.

Context: Design of OO system using mix of novices and experts.

Forces: The project consists of a large percentage of novices. Using novices everywhere, even mentored, will cause weak designs and cut & paste code.

Resolution: Separate generic from specific parts of problems. Use an expert, framework designer to design generic parts. Let the novice programmers design the specific parts.

Generics and Specifics is derived from Subsystem by Skill, and Subclass per Team. It is applicable to any technology, such as object orientation, that permits plug-in frameworks. A framework can provide a generic solution to a problem, which can be completed, extended or tailored in the specific by subclassing. The generic solution, re-siding at the higher level of the class hierarchy, is considerably more difficult to design than any one specific solution. Once programmed, it is considerably quicker and easier to complete than the specific solutions would be to design.

Therefore, use the experts' extra skill to design a generic framework solution, and use the novices to use and tailor it for a specific solution. This fits well with the Subclass by Teams principle, since the expert will be optimizing using slightly different concerns than the novice.

Generics were used in all the OO systems. In the UI system, it was used for generic displays, search collection, transaction backout, and error handling. In the domain, it was used for generic transaction, error, persistence and model behavior (see Model Hierarchy, below). In the infrastructure, it was used for error handling and the persistence mechanism. In each case, novices were able to use the generic/specific structure to accomplish their tasks in less time, and keep to a more subtle architecture than they would have thought up.

Design Decision 3: Model Hierarchy

Intent: Provide the primary subsystem teams separate design spaces.

Context: OO client design, domain objects needing persistence services.

Forces: Validation, domain, and persistence are 3 parts of any persistent domain object. They are handled by different teams.

Resolution: The class hierarchy for persistent domain classes consists of Model, to contain the common domain issues, ValidatedModel to contain the validation issues, and PersistentModel to contain the persistence issues. Model and

ValidatedModel are merged since it is a relatively small design. Different people may be responsible for each.

Model Hierarchy is derived from Subsystem by Skill, Subclass per Team, and Owner per Deliverable. *Subclass by Team provides the principle to split the root domain class into several layers.* ValidatedModel could be a separate layer, using Design Decision 4: Edits Inside. On the case study project, there were only two teams (hence two layers), and there was not enough left in Model to warrant the third layer (per the counterforce of Subclass per Team, the number of layers was not made larger than needed). An example of keeping the Model layer separate is ParcPlace's ObjectWorks class hierarchy.

Ideally, the description of the business behavior of the application should be independent of the particular persistence mechanism used, so that the persistence mechanism can be changed without damaging the business behavior. By job description and expertise, the person who knows the behavior of business objects is not likely to be the person who knows about persistence mechanisms, and vice versa.

The teams made changes to their interfaces and implementations concurrently. They had different interests, and different ideas as to what is 'best'. The subsystems were in one level initially, and fights between the groups occurred. The class also started to become a "common area" (see Owner per Deliverable). Having the 2 layers of sub-classing allowed the groups to trim their designs with minimal impact on each other.

1.8 Do you remember the key points?

Here are some points I picked out to highlight:

Chapter 1.1, "Not my job" and other virtues of bureaucracies

1. "Not my job" and "No need to know": People are really good at those.

2. "Gather together those things that change for the same reason, and separate those things that change for different reasons". This is what we manage to arrange intuitively to take care of when we think of our bureaucracy.

3. Ron Crocker made use of Conway's Law in large-scale system design: He decided the local responsibilities for each team to work on, then constrained the allowed communication paths between those subsystems and teams

Chapter 1.2, CRC cards and responsibilities:

1. CRC stands for class, responsibility, collaborator.

2. If you get a couple of people and role-play the system in action using CRC cards, you will feel, immediately, if this little bureaucracy is making sense or not.

3. if you compare the name of the object, the responsibility statement, and the data and method signatures (as one thing), you can detect if something is out of alignment.

Chapter 1.3, Anthropomorphic design with objects:

1. An object is a thing with all the state and services that come with it..

2. In *bureaucracy design*, an object is a thing with a personal secretary with a filing cabinet and a phone or fax - we decide how much knowledge and power this person has.

3. We hide the exact mechanism behind the interface, so we can change our minds later, and the client object is protected from those changes. We are keeping the "trajectory of change" low.

4. Object design is the design of how much knowledge and control goes into each object.

5. We use the "need to know" question to limit the view of the internal data. We allocate queries and commands to objects to keep their knowledge in check and reduce the trajectory of change.

6. The designer's review list: What should this object do? All of it, or delegate some? How much does it know, how much does it reveal?

Chapter 1.4, Choosing a responsibility statement:

1. The responsibility statement is the shortest description of a unit's function. It captures the size, the power of the object relative to the functioning of the system.

2. The problem with narrow responsibilities is that the design fragments so much that it loses its overall shape and is harder to understand. Later changes easily spread over multiple objects.

3. The fatness of an object's responsibility changes over time.

4. The *active* responsibilities define the architecture of the system.

5. A system documented in this way speaks clearly to its readers, allows discussion, challenge, and alternative designs to be debated.

Chapter 1.5, Using scenarios to evaluate your design:

1. Role play the workings of the system using scenarios to discover and test responsibilities.

2. Pick up the cards one by one as the bureaucracy handles the situation. Listen to your body reacting to whether what you are saying out loud makes sense to you.

3. When you feel it is off, see it is the name, the responsibility or the data and methods. Any one of them could be off.

4. Consider business changes and see what you have to change. What-ifs let you stress test your design.

From Chapter 1.6, Diagramming interactions:

1. Show the interactions in top view or time view.

2. Top view has good visual mnemonic value (it has a "shape") and is good for overall system documentation.

3. Top view doesn't scale and is not so good for examining details of the interactions.

4. Time view is good for staring at the detailed interactions to make sure they are correct.

5. Time view does not have a "shape" and has low mnemonic value.

6. My 3-step iterative design technique:
   CRC cards. Time-view the interactions. Code. Restart lol.

7. Use the diagrams to help you think through your design and to communicate it to another person

From Chapter 1.7, Inheritance and generic responsibilities

1. Treat two layers of an inheritance hierarchy as two objects, where the upper layer handles the generic parts and the lower layer handles the case-specific situations.

2. They are two different people in the bureaucracy, with those responsibilities: generic and specific.
   Say out loud, "Generically, the client asks for this…" and "In this specific case, we also need to…"

3. Extra credit: Subclass or instance variable?
    Subclass if you expect never to change it.
    if you plan on changing it, prefer an instance variable.

Part 2: Examples of designs

Here is a deeper dive into three designs to see how they allocate responsibilities, and to learn to talk about these designs in terms of a bureaucracy.

2.1 Model-View-Controller and variations

Intention

I had the luck to spend a year in Oslo working with Trygve Reenskaug, inventor of Model-View-Controller. I can't find a reference to this story to it as he told me, so I will relate what he said as I recall it.

> *In the early and mid 1970s, Trygve had been working in Norway on designing large ships for the Norwegian navy. One of the problems was the amount and diversity of the data. They had interrelated design aspects from the structure, the shape, the electrical network, plumbing, colors, cost and so on.*
>
> *Trygve got a chance to go and work on the relatively new Smalltalk-74 system at the Xerox Palo Alto Research Center (PARC), where he would be the first outsider applying Smalltalk to a real problem.*
>
> *To work with the different aspects of a ship, Trygve decided that each aspect should have its code in different places. The code for looking at the electrical layout should reside in a different place than the code for looking at the structural, plumbing or color aspects.*

In terms of the bureaucratic model, the parts showing the electrical layout had no "need to know" about the structural aspects. The ship itself - the core domain data - had to have all the aspects, electrical, structural, plumbing and so on, but the view at any one time could be specialized. In terms of the bureaucracy, it's "not my job", says the core domain data, "to know how the user wants this presented on the screen, or on paper, perhaps in a report."

Trygve therefore separated the View classes according to these aspects, and separated those from the Model.

Finally, he decided to separate the responsibility of showing how something looked from making changes. Why should the visual presentation know about the mouse clicks and requests to change the model? So he separated out the Controller, whose job it is to make changes to the model.

Here is how that looks, with responsibilities:

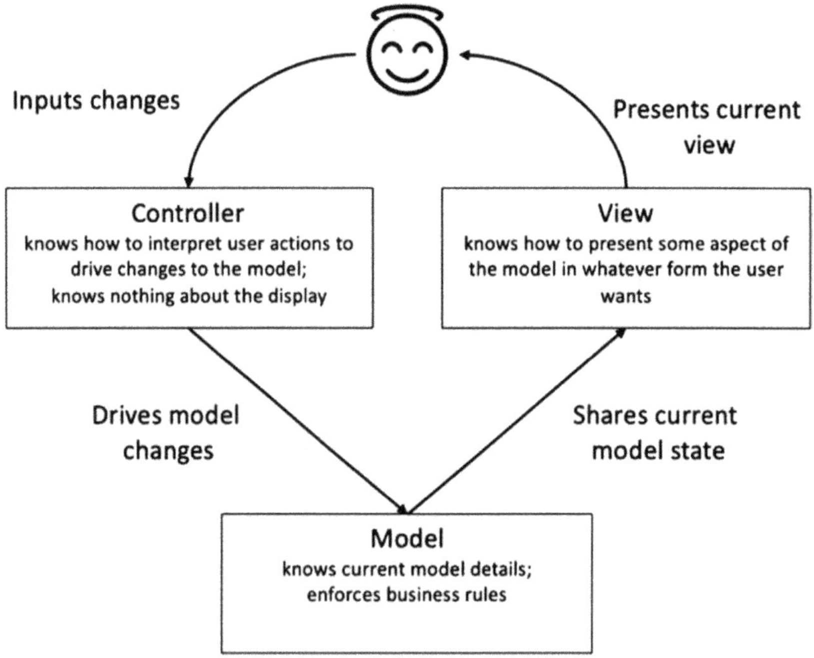

Figure 26. Model-View-Controller with responsibilities.

In the running system, he could look at the electrical and structural aspects side by side. Since each view only worked with the details it needed to know about, the code base was tidy. When something changed in the core model, all views were updated simultaneously to show the resulting effect.

Model-View-Controller and the "generic" argument

Many beginners find the MVC framework difficult, because the superclass layers interact with each other in complicated ways, guaranteeing certain great behaviors, but not obvious just how.

Key among these is the way that view updates are done.

- The programmer creates a new model class as a subclass of Model and a new view class as a subclass of View.

- Unseen to this programmer, because it is in the MVC framework, when a new view and model are created, the view's superclass sends a message to the model, saying, "Let me know when you change" or "Let me know when this aspect of you changes".

- The model superclass knows to store the location of the view. When that aspect of the model changes, it sends a message to the view saying, "I changed" (nothing more).

- The subclass, not the superclass (remember they are two different people in the bureaucracy?) picks up that message and asks the specific model (the subclass) to give it the details it is interested in.

<u>The two superclass elements have the responsibility to carry out the generic parts of the MVC conversation; the subclasses have no need to know exactly how that is done.</u>

The subclass elements have to do nothing during setup (that's the freaky part). They only pick up the "I changed" message and ask for information at that time.

What makes this difficult for a beginning programmer is that the communication between the generic View and the generic Model are hidden and fairly subtle, especially in the setup period.

Here is the time view of the interactions, so you can see how the superclasses set up the conversation:

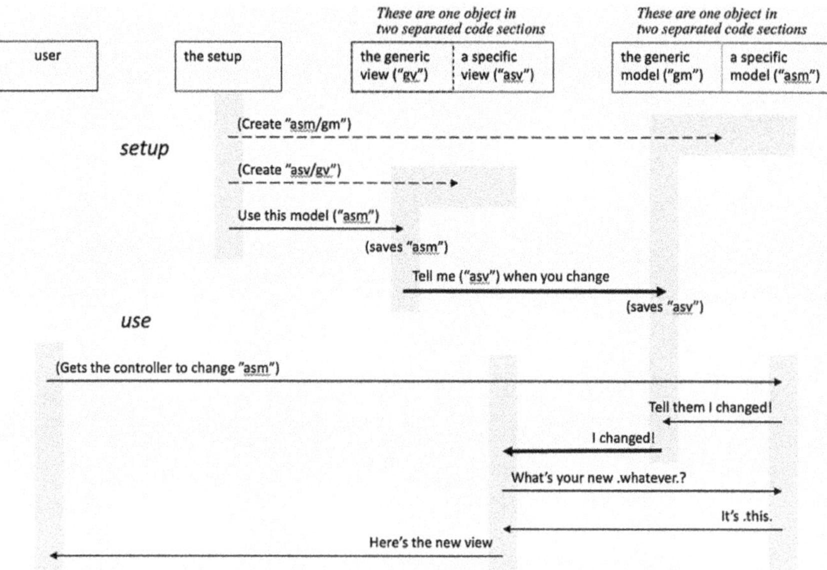

Figure 27. MVC timeline showing inherited behavior.

In that diagram, I split the model and view objects into their two parts: The superclass, which comes as part of the MVC package, is on the left. The subclass on the right. Although in operation there is only one object, the code resides in two different spaces, so it's not easy to see how the two parts collaborate.

In the drawing, the gray verticals show when they each are active. The two parts of the object get created at the same time (of course). The superclass parts are active during setup, and at just one moment during use. What is confusing for the beginning programmer is that the subclass parts do nothing during setup. The subclass code "merely" picks up "I changed" and goes and gets the needed data. Magic.

The Model-Interactor variant

The reason I described Trygve's motivation for creating the MVC pattern is because not many of us work with a domain model so complicated that we need different types of views at the same time. For most projects, it is just too much.

People complained: "Why do we have these two classes (view and controller), when in my situation they both change together?" Or: "This is too bureaucratic. Too many handoffs."

Someone decided to merge the View with the Controller and call the combined pair an Interactor. The Model-Interactor framework is simpler and sensible in these other situations.

My point in mentioning the Model-Interactor is to show a case in which responsibilities were split apart in one situation, and merged back again in a different situation. It is not always better to have more objects with more granular responsibilities.

The overly-controlling-controller variant

I haven't used MVC for ages, so I was surprised and shocked when I looked it up online for this writing. One of the popular variants has what I consider much too much responsibility in the controller.

When I saw this diagram, I immediately asked: "Why is the controller asking for details about the change of state? That's none of its business!"

Followed by, "That controller is taking over the conversation too much. It should at most connect two objects that need to know about each other and then get out of the way."

Did you ever have a conversation online where person A should introduce you to person B, but doesn't actually introduce you two? Person A just plays relay between the two of you, tells you what B said, tells B what you said?

Don't you get tired of that? I mean, just introduce you to B and just let the two of you get the conversation going. Why should A keep intercepting the messages in each direction and shuttle them on? That just causes delays.

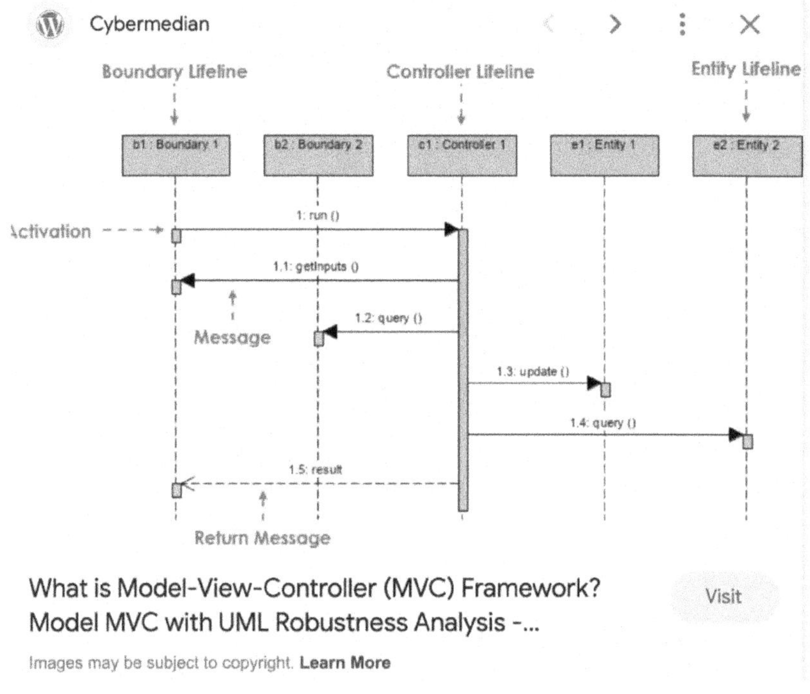

Figure 28. The controller in this version knows about the view.

Additionally, in this design, when the needs of the view change, the programmer also has to change the controller. Seems like an unnecessary number of objects for a change.

There was surely a good reason to make this design in its context. My purpose here is how I use the bureaucracy model to analyze a design.

Postscript: In the Wikipedia article, it says: "Smalltalk-80... If user input prompts a change in a model, the controller will signal the model to change, but the model is then responsible for telling its views to update." Then: "In WebObjects, the views handle user input, and the controller mediates between the views and the models."

[https://en.wikipedia.org/wiki/Model%E2%80%93view%E2%80%93controller]
[https://www.visual-paradigm.com/guide/uml-unified-modeling-language/how-to-model-mvc-with-uml-sequence-diagram/]
[https://www.visual-paradigm.com/guide/uml-unified-modeling-language/what-is-model-view-control-mvc/]

2.2 The "Squeegee" technique

This is a technique I used once when two design teams couldn't agree on a design. The example is really detailed because <u>I wish to show how design is done with careful attention to "who knows what."</u>

> *We had a 3-tier system with a client workstation running an OO application, connected to a Unix server / database, and a mainframe / database. We couldn't decide what sort of database would be used on the Unix server: object or relational. Our initial guess was relational.*
>
> *<u>The developers had a tendency to design persistent objects that looked mostly like relational tables</u>. Their discussions were full of references to the tables. This was natural, given the presence of the relational database then being used on the server, and the need to normalize the database.*
>
> *It made the experts nervous, both out of our sense as purists, and also because we were afraid that the server database might suddenly be switched to objects. The design of the workstation object would lose the resiliency offered by OO design. Every change in the server would causes a change in the domain classes, which might cause a change in its client, a large trajectory of change.*
>
> *We sought a pattern of thinking for the newcomers so that relational tables would not enter into their discussions, and they would produce designs based on other reasoning.*

The situation came to a crisis with the design of the Account class that we just saw in the discussion on inheritance. It was complex, needed to be stored on the server, and cached of intermediate results. It had been redesigned several times and the team leads were losing their ability to work through the design carefully and impartially. Time was short, as were tempers.

More than just a design, <u>we needed a way to talk that would get agreement at every intermediate stage</u>, so that the different experts would not simply disagree with the end result. It should produce a legitimate design not based on relational table structure, so that we could cut over to an object database without trauma. A technique that could be passed to the newcomer designers for their use and, additionally, so that the experts would agree with their reasoning.

Making matters worse, the sales force in the field was dialing into headquarters over 9600 baud phone lines. (Sorry for the ancient reference, 9600 baud means 9,600 bits per second! None of this megabits/second stuff. We're talking.... slow.)

The sales force wanted to see summaries of the checking accounts: sales by month, by geographic area, and by area by month. It was up to the server programmers to decide whether the summaries were calculated on the fly or stored, but the workstation needed to cache the summaries, because of those 9600 baud phone lines.

In debating solutions, we found we were saying things "because it is on the database anyway," "because it is / is not object-oriented," "because it violates encapsulation," and so on. None of these are very convincing arguments.

We eventually found a way to lock one section of the design space and "squeegee" the rest into a smaller space. Each time we secured a section of the design space, some designers would be able to design in peace, knowing that design changes in the other sections wouldn't affect them. "Reduce the trajectory of change" was our motto.

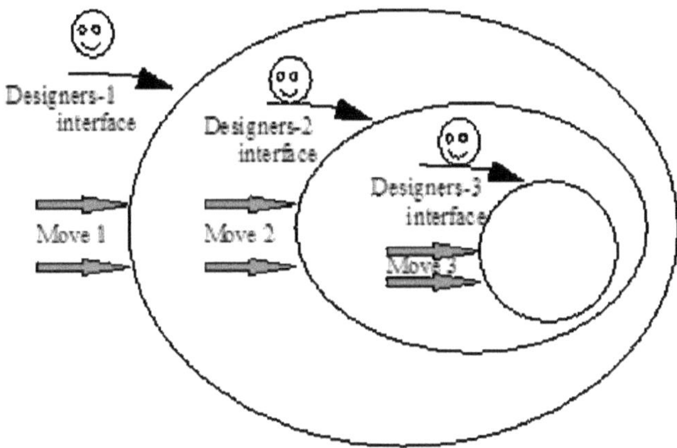

Figure 29. The basic squeegee technique.

The area of most contention was the server design, so we wanted that to be the last move, corresponding to the inside circle in Figure 29. The objects on the workstation should not care what server technology was used. More importantly, if ever the workstation business object knew anything about the server, its clients should not know.

So, we created four zones of design:

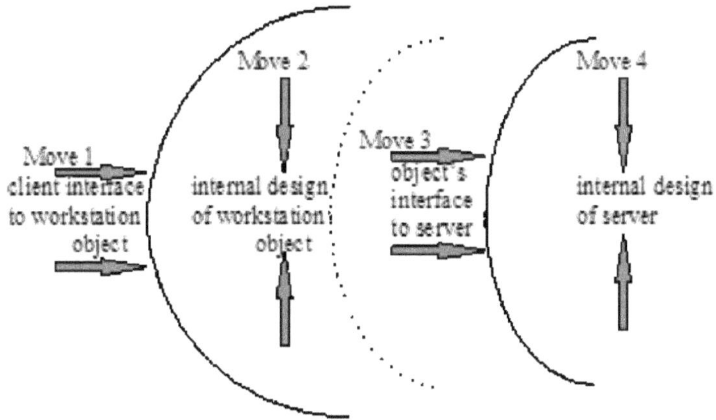

Figure 30. Client-server design in four moves.

In the first move, we concentrated on the dialog between the domain object and its clients. We wanted to ensure they had a suitable interface and their dialog was independent of the server technology. This part was easy.

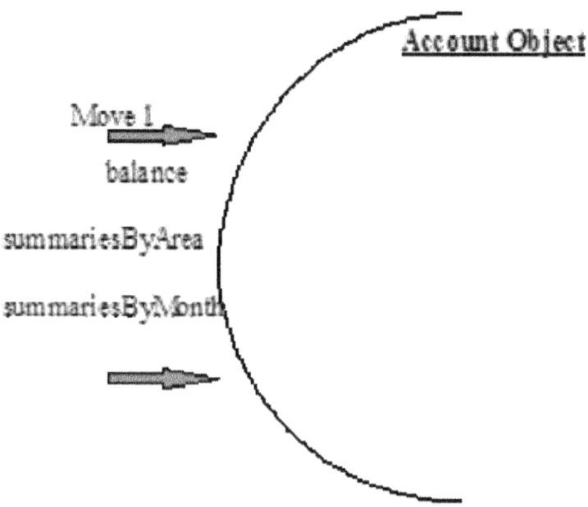

Figure 31. Move 1 secures the workstation object's client interface.

After move one, the object's clients no longer cared about the details of distribution, the nature of the server database. The design of that interface was sound and stable.

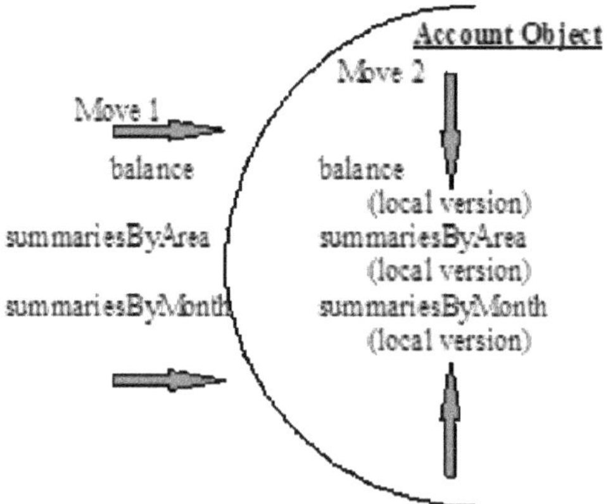

Figure 32. Move 2 secures the workstation object's internal design.

Move two was to pretend all processing was local, there was no server. We asked, "What would be a sound local design?"

This wasn't quite so easy, because we had to deal with the summaries that might be out of sync with the server. Even assuming a fast, local processor and large amounts of local memory, we decided it made sense to create summary objects rather than recompute the summaries every time the user opened a window. Assuming the software would work entirely from local memory, we decided the design would consist of the classes: Account, Transaction, SummaryByArea, SummaryByMonth, SummaryByTypeByMonth.

So Account had a local storage variable for the current balance, and knew two collections, its summariesByAreas and summariesByMonths. It did not need to know all of its Transactions, nor SummariesByTypeByMonths, which SummaryByMonth would know. Only SummaryByArea and SummaryByTypeByMonth would know of Transactions directly. See the figure below.

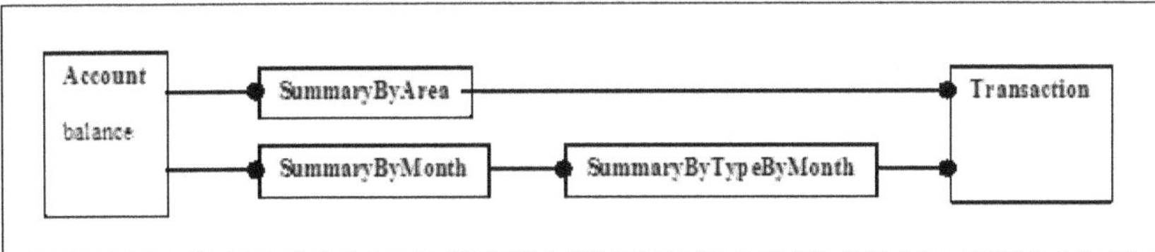

Figure 33. Diagram of the workstation classes.

These decisions made sense in the context of local processing, independently of the server design. Since we didn't touch the server design, the server designers couldn't disagree. End of move two.

In move three, we added the facts of distribution, allowing for performance loss through delays and multiple, concurrent users. This required more considerations:

In distributing the services, we could choose to have the server deliver all the transactions and let the workstation do the adding to build the summaries, or we could choose to have the server build the summaries. In a situation where transmission speed were not a problem, as on a local area network, we might have chosen to let the workstation do the addition, to off-load the server. However, with those slow telephone lines, minimizing transmission traffic was paramount.

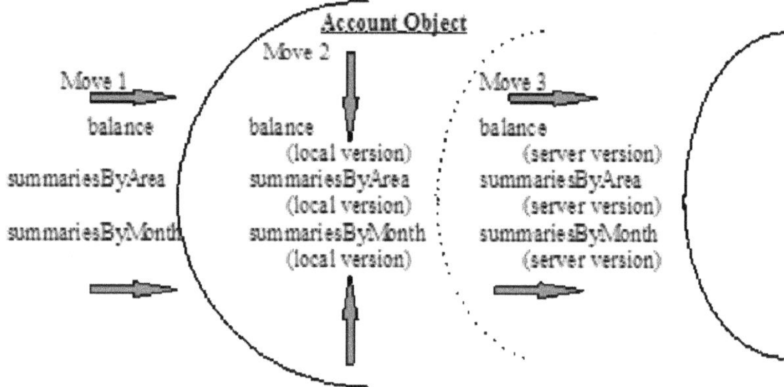

Figure 34. Move 3 secures the server's service interface.

Therefore, we decided that the server should support the exact services the workstation needed, namely balance, summariesByArea, summariesByMonth, and so on. This was not a hard decision for both groups of designers to agree to.

Is everything the same? Has anything at all changed with the distribution? There is a subtle but significant difference. Recall that many people were working on different workstations at the same time. When any one user requested the balance or a summary, the server guaranteed the freshness of the answer. That answer became out of date as other users added transactions. The balance and summaries on each workstation reflected the changes made on that workstation, but not the changes the other users made.

Although "balance" on the workstation and "balance" as a service from the server sound the same, they have different meanings, and carried different values. It was difficult for us to get used to the idea that the balance variable on the workstation and the balance from the server were actually different.

What we had established at this point is that the workstation stored such a variable rather than recomputing it every time, but we had not established whether such a storage exists on the server. The surprise was that the workstation designers did not have to care. "Not their job", "No need to know."

To deal with the staleness of the data on the workstation in the presence of multiple users, we changed the client interface to add one more function, "refresh". When the user pressed the "Refresh" button, the workstation object would go out to the server to get up-to-date values.

At this point we were actually already done. The server programmers guaranteed to provide the workstation with the promised data, the workstation programmers would not care whether the server uses a relational or object database, or whether data was stored or recomputed. The workstation team was now on its way.

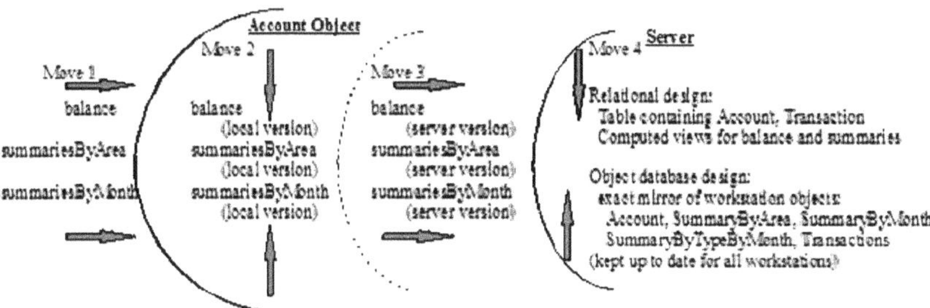

Figure 35. Move 4 settles the server's implementation.

Let's finish the story:

The server team started with a relational database. They decided that the balance and the summaries would be computed on the fly. That kept the database clean, and guaranteed fresh data on every request. For about half a year, we were uncertain whether they would change the server to use an object database. In the end, they didn't, but nobody worried about that any more.

This was how we used "no need to know" and "not my job" from the outer layers inwards at each step to close out a contentious design problem.

2.3 Hexagonal architecture

I invented the "hexagonal" architecture because I was tired of getting burned. It turned out to solve a colleague's problem and saved some headaches on another project, so I turned it into a pattern.

The hexagonal architecture pattern is described at length on the web and in a full book on the subject.

[https://alistair.cockburn.us/hexagonal-architecture/]

[https://hexagonalarchitecture.org/]

[https://alistaircockburn.company.site/Epub-Hexagonal-Architecture-Explained-Updated-1st-ed-p751233517/].

In what follows, I focus on the bureaucracy, responsibilities, "not my job", "no need to know" and so on.

A standard design that causes trouble

The usual way to get started is to make three subsystems:

- The UI, which knows details of how to present information and collect user intentions,

- The Application, which knows the business rules and how to enforce them, plus the business model, how to use and update it,

- Some repository, which keeps the data safe; provides data as needed and accepts changes.

All seems very natural so far.

What happens is that people start putting bits of the UI into the application, detailed knowledge of the repository structure in the application, bits of the business logic in the UI, and so on.

That is, the responsibility allocation may have been fine to start with, but there is just no enforcement of it, so it goes wrong.

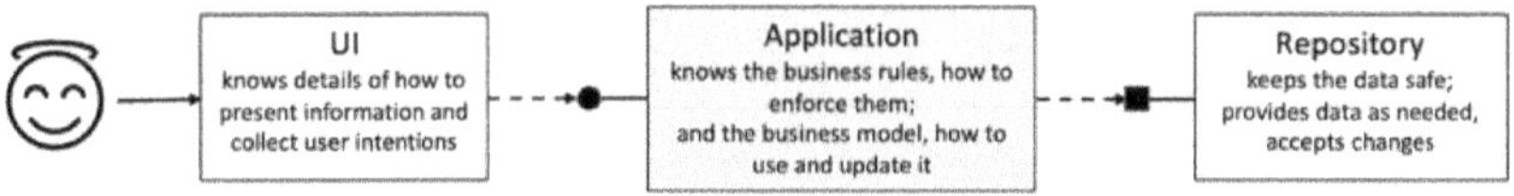

Figure 36. The standard 3-layer architecture causes trouble.

In the above figure, the solid circle and square indicate the interfaces the callers must use. The dashed arrow means the calling object uses that interface. We will see more of these coming up.

It turns out there is a second problem, particularly on the repository side: There is nothing in the responsibility allocation that says that the application *shouldn't* know anything about the repository formats. (Well, we might imagine that it shouldn't, but staring at the programming screen, it all seems so natural, right?).

It is hard to make good regression tests of the application, since the application is coupled tightly with the repository.

So far, there is no terrible damage, and teams continue to design, maintain, evolve systems like these for years.

Over time, though, technology changes. If the programmers didn't keep the responsibility separations squeaky clean, <u>suddenly new UI or repository technologies trigger changes throughout the code base</u>, not just in the ideally located spots.

It gets worse, even with a tidy separation. I'll tell just the one story from the project after which I decided I really had to formalize this pattern. It comes from Project Winifred, described at length in *Surviving Object-Oriented Projects*.

> *1994. We were on a cutting edge project matching a Smalltalk UI and business logic implementation with a relational database and some COBOL programs. The people responsible for writing the code that would get back and forth between Smalltalk objects and the tables were excellent programmers, working under hefty time pressure to make something new and difficult.*

> *Their first design did an OK job. They ran into two problems: each class and request had to be hand coded, and there would be*

too many of them, so they really needed a framework. Then, when they did that, the round-trip time to the database was too slow, so they had to redesign their framework from scratch, with a different interface to the business logic.

All programming came to a screeching halt while they changed that interface. It took weeks for them to develop a brand new interface.

I asked for a "loopback" mechanism, what we now call an in-memory repository or a test double, so the domain programmers could make their own test data and keep going while the new framework was being designed.

The infrastructure designers looked at me like I had three heads and said, "No."

That cost the project several weeks of down time, with a dozen domain programmers sitting idle.

Why did this happen? It happened because the interface between the domain code and the repository driver, residing in the domain superclass, knew too much about the details of the database and couldn't be replaced with a substitute.

Tighten the responsibilities

The way forward is to tighten the responsibilities a bit.

<u>The application refuses to talk to anyone except in its preferred internal language</u>. That pushes the responsibility for matching vocabularies outward, to "someone else". But whom?

The UI screen says, "Not my job to know what the domain language is, I'm all about screen things."

The repository says, "Not my job to know what the domain language is, I'm all about relational tables things (or JSON, or whatever)."

So, we have to introduce an adapter, whose responsibility is is to know both the screen language and the domain language; or the domain language and the repository language.

It turns out that UML already accounts for this seemingly strange situation: "provided" and "required" interfaces.

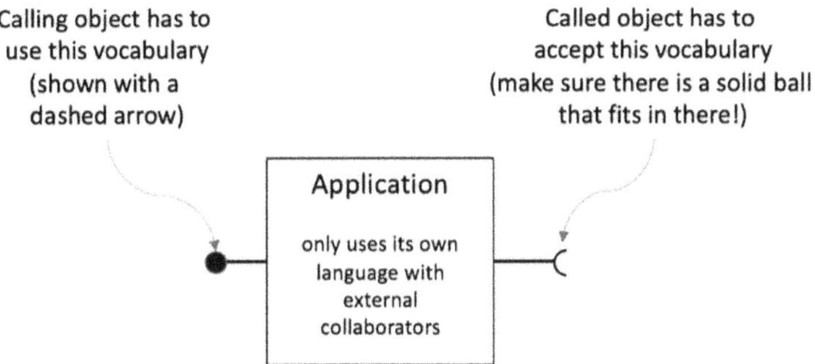

Figure 37. UML conventions for provided and required interfaces.

The *provided interface* is the interface the application offers to whatever wants to make a request of it. That is the little ball we saw earlier. It is totally normal, it's just every function call you've ever used.

The *required interface* is the interface the component *demands that another object offers* as its provided interface! That is less normal. It is really ego-centric of the application to require that the repository accept service calls in the way the application designers want. The required interface is shown as a C-shaped socket jutting out from the object.

The repository typically comes from a vendor, so the application programmers don't get to change it. If we need that adapter, we have to write it ourselves. We can arrange for it to honor the application's required interface, and translate that to the language of the repository.

Our design now looks like this:

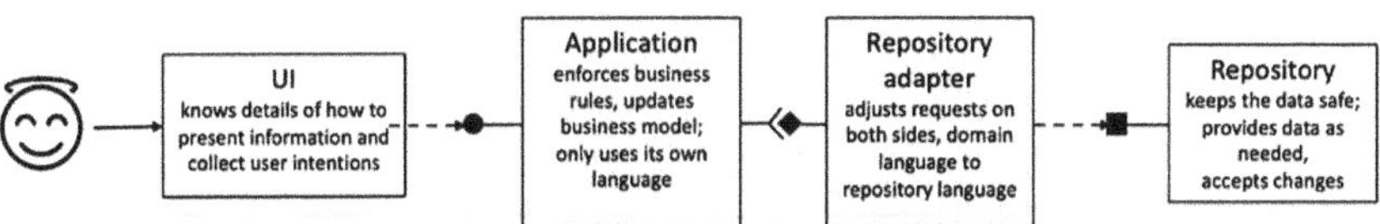

Figure 38. Architecture with adapters around the domain.

We have to write the coupling of the GUI framework to our application's provided interface, and we have to write the adapter that maps the application's preferred way of asking for things - its required interface - to the repository's provided interface.

In this picture, I use three different connector shapes to show the three different interfaces. The repository adapter must define the same provided interface that the application requires, and uses the (different) interface that the repository expects.

What happens next is interesting.

Once we have the application sitting in its own little beautiful world, talking only in its own language, we can substitute different adapters for different technologies. Migrating the UI technology is easy, shifting to a new repository technology is easy. And for my poor project Winifred, *letting the domain programmers substitute in their own local test cases is easy!*

But wait, there's more!

Since the application is tightly encapsulated on all sides, testing suddenly becomes easier. We can write full system-function tests on all sides, using a test harness on the driver side a test double on the repository side.

But wait, there's more! A new possibility now opens up, that wasn't there before:

Those tests can enforce the rule that no UI or repository details get into the business logic and no business logic gets into the UI or repository. Should anyone figure a bit of business logic into the UI, the tests will break.

And so we come full circle: We can enforce the separation of responsibilities that we asked for at the beginning.

Here is a picture showing a generic driver and external system, with a swappable test double. We can switch between test double and database whenever we want, build or run time.

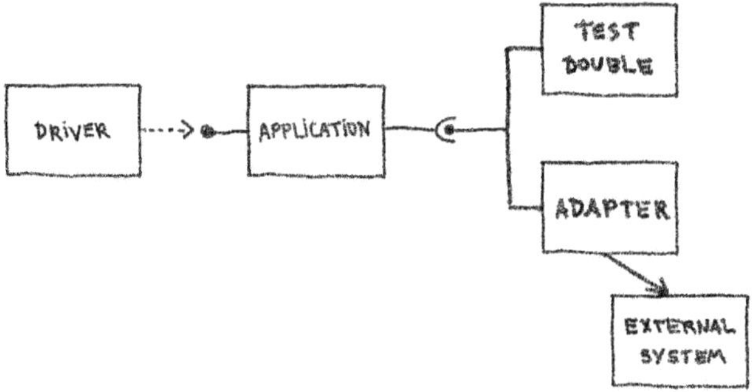

Figure 39. The architecture with test double, adapter and repository.

The last mystery

Wait, there's a dangling mystery: Why is this called "hexagonal architecture"? I don't see a hexagon anywhere!

Ah, well, you see, I didn't know all of these terms in 1999 when I first showed this to a colleague, or in 2005 when I first wrote it up.

All I knew was it had to be this way. Responsibilities and all that. So I drew a hexagon. I wanted to break the habit of top-bottom, and hang multiple things off different places. So I drew a hexagon, what the heck.

It works quite well, as in this fairly complicated system:

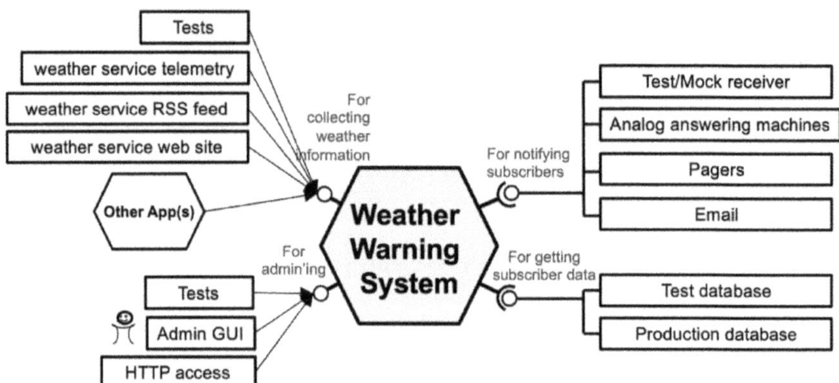

Figure 40. Hexagonal architecture with several ports.

The correct name for this pattern is *Ports and Adapters*. It is described in detail in the book *Hexagonal Architecture Explained* (2025) as well as "Component-plus-Strategy generalizes Ports-and-Adapters", the articles that contains the newer language:

[https://alistaircockburn.com/Articles/Component-Strategy-generalizes-Ports-Adapters]

We still call it hexagonal architecture because it's more fun. But really, it's all about ports and adapters.

2.4 Do you remember the key points?

Here are some points I picked out to highlight:

Chapter 2.1 Model-View-Controller and variations

1. the parts showing the electrical layout had no "need to know" about the structural aspects.

2. it's "not my job", says the core domain data, "to know how the user wants this presented."

3. Trygve therefore separated the View classes according to these aspects, and separated those from the Model.

4. Since each view only worked with the details it needed to know about, the code base was tidy.

5. The two superclass parts have the responsibility to carry out the generic parts of the MVC conversation; the subclasses have no need to know exactly how that is done.

6. It is not always better to have more objects with more granular responsibilities.

7. "Why is the controller asking for details about the change of state? That's none of its business!"

8. My intention here is to how I use the bureacracy model to analyze a design.

Chapter 2.2 The "Squeegee" technique

1. I wish to show how design is done with careful attention to "who knows what."

2. The developers had a tendency to design persistent objects that looked mostly like relational tables. …

3. we needed a way to talk that would get agreement at every intermediate stage.

4. "Reduce the trajectory of change" was our motto.

5. The objects on the workstation should not care what server technology was used.

6. we created four zones of design.

7. After move one, the object's clients no longer cared about the details of distribution.

8. Since we didn't touch the server design, the server designers couldn't disagree. End of move two.

9. In move three, we added the facts of distribution.

10. Although "balance" on the workstation and "balance" as a service from the server sound the same, they have different meanings, and carried different values.

11. we had not established whether such a storage exists on the server. The surprise was that the workstation designers did not have to care. "Not their job", "No need to know."

12. At this point we were actually already done.

Chapter 2.3 Hexagonal architecture

1. the responsibility allocation may have been fine to start with, but there is just no enforcement of it,so it goes wrong.

2. suddenly new UI or repository technologies trigger changes throughout the code base.

3. The application refuses to talk to anyone except in its preferred internal language.

4. The *required interface* is the interface the component *demands that another object offers* as its provided interface.

5. Once we have the application sitting in its own little beautiful world, talking only in its own language, we can substitute different adapters for different technologies.

6. Those tests can enforce the rule that no UI or repository details get into the business logic.

7. The correct name for this pattern is *Ports and Adapters*.

Part 3: Three More Techniques

Twenty percent of the technique gets you eighty percent of the value. You just got that juicy twenty percent, and what to know what's next.

The most important next technique to learn is to "grow" your programs.

The second is the Walking Skeleton pattern (The first step in growing programs).

Beyond that, investigate other fascinating design techniques. I include here a reference to "deriving your programs," an obscure and rarely-needed but insanely powerful technique when you do need it.

3.1 Nano-incremental development: Grow your design

Along with "Where do I put this line of code?" a core skill to develop is "growing" your system in nano-increments.

First described by Harlan Mills as "growing" in 1971, it was publicized in 1975 by Vic Basili as "iterative enhancement" and finally declared a best practice by Fred Brooks in his "No Siver Bullet" article.

Here is Fred Brooks:

> *"Some years ago Harlan Mills proposed that any software system should be* grown *by incremental development [1]. That is, the system should first be made to run, even though it does nothing useful except call the proper set of dummy subprograms. Then, bit by bit it is fleshed out, with the subprograms in turn being developed into actions or calls to empty stubs in the level below.*
>
> *I have seen most dramatic results since I began urging this technique on the project builders in my Software Engineering Laboratory class. Nothing in the past decade has so radically changed my own practice, or its effectiveness. The approach necessitates top-down design, for it is a top-down growing of the software. It allows easy backtracking. It lends itself to early prototypes. Each added function and new provision for more complex data or circumstances grows organically out of what is already there.*
>
> *The morale effects are startling. Enthusiasm jumps when there is a running system, even a simple one. Efforts redouble when the first picture from a new graphics software system appears on the screen, even if it is only a rectangle. One always has, at every stage in the process, a working system. I find that teams can grow much more complex entities in four months than they can build.*
>
> *The same benefits can be realized on large projects as on my small ones.*

In 1986 when that paper came out, I had no idea what he was talking about. My office mate, who was a very good programmer, said, "Oh, that's how I work all the time."

Although it took over a decade for me to learn how to do it, it is now is my standard way of working. The "Elephant Carpaccio" exercise is designed to teach both why and how to grow a system using nano-incremental development.

I detail the advantages of incremental development in full detail in *The Book on Fine-Grained Incremental Development*. It contains separate chapters for sponsoring executive, the business person, the product manager, the project manager, and the programmer.

Mastering the skill of "growing" your system is, in my mind, even more important than designing with responsibilities (which is why I wrote that book).

References:

1. Mills, H. D. "Top-down programming in large systems," *Debugging Techniques in Large Systems*, R. Rustin, ed., Englewood Cliffs, N.J., Prentice-Hall, 1971.

2. Victor R. Basili and Albert J. Turner, "Iterative Enhancement: A Practical Technique for Software Development," IEEE Transactions on Software Engineering, Vol. SE-1, No.4, December 1975. [https://ieeexplore.ieee.org/document/6312870]

3. "No Silver Bullet – Essence and accident in software engineering," Fred Brooks, 1986. [https://www.cs.unc.edu/techreports/86-020.pdf]

4. A Cockburn, *The Book on Fine-Grained Incremental Development*," 2026.

5. The "Elephant Carpaccio" exercise: [https://alistaircockburn.com/Elephant-Carpaccio]

3.2 The Walking Skeleton pattern

*A **Walking Skeleton** is a tiny implementation of the system that performs a small end-to-end function. It need not use the final architecture, but it should link together the main architectural components. The architecture and the functionality can then evolve in parallel.*

The first step in growing a program is to create a Walking skeleton. I learned this technique in a casual conversation in the early 1990s and wrote it up after I used it and saw others using it to good advantage.

Vic Basili and Albert Turner described exactly this in 1975:

"Furthermore, design flaws often do not show up until the implementation is well underway so that correcting the problems can require major effort.

One practical approach to this problem is to start with a simple initial implementation of a subset of the problem and iteratively enhance existing versions until the full system is implemented. At each step of the process, not only extensions but also design modifications can be made. In fact, each step can make use of stepwise refinement in a more effective way as the system becomes better understood through the iterative process. As these iterations converge to the full solution, fewer and fewer modifications need be made. "Iterative enhancement" represents a practical means of applying stepwise refinement.

The first step in the application of the iterative enhancement technique to a software development project consists of a simple initial implementation of a skeletal subproblem of the project.

Connect the major architectural components, the user interface or driving program and the main repository or external connection.

Consider putting a kiosk in a store so say where an item is located and whether it is in stock. The kiosk has to connect to the existing inventory management system, a tricky and high-risk connection Connecting early is of great value to the project, even if only simplest request is implemented.

The walking skeleton for this system connects the three components:

- a simple user interface on some device,
- the location app,
- the inventory management system.

Program only a fixed request (I always choose Bob Marley's *Legend* album 😊). The UI sends that request to the app, which implements only that one request of the inventory management system.

Keep the interfaces and the programming as simple as possible. Prove that the connections work and to flush out surprises in the connections. They will all get revised over time as they are grown.

Connecting these elements does two good things for the project:

- It reduces a huge amount of risk, because connecting external technologies is fraught with hidden obstacles and errors;
- It allows the infrastructure team and the function-developing teams to work in parallel.

The cost, of course, is rework. The architecture is likely to drift, and the interfaces certainly will. However, experience

The *Walking Skeleton* pattern is described on my old website and in detail in *The Book on Fine-Grained Incremental Development.*

References:

1. The Walking Skeleton pattern:
   [https://web.archive.org/web/20140329201356/http://alistair.cockburn.us/Walking+skeleton]
2. "Iterative Enhancement: A Practical Technique for Software Development," Victor R. Basili and Albert J. Turner, IEEE Transactions on Software Engineering, Vol. SE-1, No.4, December 1975. [https://ieeexplore.ieee.org/document/6312870]
3. *The Book on Fine-Grained Incremental Development*, A. Cockburn, 2026.

3.3 Deriving your program

In the 1970s, Edsger Dijkstra produced some remarkable algorithms we still use today, using an even more remarkable technique: deriving, not inventing, algorithms.

He constructed a simple non-deterministic guarded-clause logic with which he could quite literally deduce from a stated post-condition how a correct program should look.

David Gries made it accessible to practitioners in 1981 with his book *The Science of Programming*.

This technique serves perfectly for algorithm design. The code it produces is incredibly tight, and most remarkably, works correctly the first time.

It does not address "Where do I put this line of code?" because the topics it addresses are typically small and reside in one or two functions.

I had the pleasure of using the technique a few times, the most difficult of which was programming a fast line-drawing algorithm in assembler with loops unrolled, jumping into and out of the unrolled loops as the line progressed.

It was clear that I would never be able to debug that code and keep it both correct and tight, so I spent an entire day deriving it. I typed it in, and it worked straight off. Remarkable.

I won't try to describe the technique here. You can still buy Gries's book and find Dijkstra's writing online. Fascinating reading and a great if obscure programming technique for those rare moments when you need it.

References:

1. *The Science of Programming*, David Gries, Springer Verlag, 1981. [https://www.amazon.com/Science-Programming-Monographs-Computer/dp/0387964800]

2. [https://www.cs.cornell.edu/gries/TechReports/90-1102.pdf]

3. The full collection of Dijkstra papers.
   [https://www.cs.utexas.edu/~EWD/]

4. "Guarded commands. non-determinacy and a calculus for the derivation of programs"
   [https://www.cs.utexas.edu/~EWD/transcriptions/EWD04xx/EWD418.html]

4. "Nondeterminacy and Formal Derivation of Programs," Edsger W. Dijkstra Burroughs Corporation, 1974
   [https://www.cs.toronto.edu/~chechik/courses05/csc410/readings/dijkstra.pdf]

3.4. Using AI

In March 2026, we are still in the stage of wildly experimenting with AI tools that are changing every month. Therefore, and with no apologies, I'm not going to say anything much useful about the use of AI in your programming. Even if I were an expert now, whatever I write will be largely obsolete within a year. I can, however, offer this line of thinking:

The models are being loaded with all books, probably including this one. That means you can ask it for certain types of designs. *Domain-driven design* is already well established, so it should do a decent job of finding domain objects.

As we have seen, however, not all domain models make good software designs. The trajectory of change is different for different choices of domain concepts.

You should be able to ask your AI tool

- to evaluate the trajectory of change for different changes;
- to evaluate your/its design with respect to the bureaucracy model, "not my job" and "no need to know;"
- to ask it for different numbers of core domain objects, and to evaluate the comprehensibility of having so many (for having possibly too many) versus the comprehensibility or cost of change for having possibly too few.

By the time you read this, the tools will be strong enough to evaluate its designs along different axes.

My goal with this book is not just to educate you on these concepts, but give you language so that you can steer the tool in dialog.

Exercises for the Interested

Here are some exercises to warm you up. All of these exercises are intended to ask you to seek simplicity in your designs.

1. Design an actual physical bank. How would you document it on just one page?

This has always been my warmup exercises in classes, to get people to think about how they tell someone else the design of something. In this case, I choose a tiny bank, something that sits out in the remote of nowhere. This simplifying choice is just so that you don't get too fancy.

In your own way, however you like, design, is a small, one-branch bank. The whole thing, not just the computer part. Take no more than 15 minutes. Ideally, work with someone else so you can hear your conversation and turn ideas around.

Capture the design on a single sheet of paper or two half-page docs or drawings. You should be able to show this piece of paper to pretty much anyone on the street, and they would recognize the basic design of the bank.

When you are done, look at what you chose to expose in that small space that would describe your bank.

- What elements did you select to show?

Show it to someone else, and see what they don't understand, as indicators of how they think.

2. The coffee machine.

Another super simple design, very old school. Let's put it into a storyline :

> *You and I just won a bid for the software of a custom coffee vending machine for the employees of Acme Fijet Works to use on*

their lunch and coffee breaks. (Arnold, the owner, like so many programmers, just won't use something that already exists - but that's okay for our story). He wants his own, custom software.

Arnold tells us he wants a simple machine. It should serves coffee for 35 cents (a quarter and a dime, in U.S. currency). The buyer can add cream or sugar. That's all. He expects us to be able to put this little machine together quickly and for little cost.

We get together and decide there will be a coin slot, coin return lever, coin return slot, and four buttons: black, white, black with sugar, white with sugar.

That's the external design.

- What objects will you want in the software to run this machine?

- What are their responsibilities? What are their interactions?

- How do you feel about those as you role-play the system in operation?

I propose you draft your first design before you turn the page for some more thoughts and questions.

Note: Yes, in 2025+ you can vibe-code this thing in a heartbeat, but lets learn how to construct the objects. When you take a larger problem, you'll know how to dialog with your agent.

Did you consider the various scenarios, including failure scenarios.

Here are two sample questions I would ask you:

- Which component knows the price of the drink?

- Which component knows how to make the drink?

Here are five scenarios I can think of. Did you think of these? How does your system handle them? Role-play the scenarios and see how you feel.

1. Kim puts in a quarter and then selects a coffee.

2. Kim puts two quarters in and then selects a coffee.

3. Kim puts in a quarter, then pushes the coin return lever.

4. Kim puts in a two quarters, then walks away from the machine and forgets to come back.

5. Kim buys two coffees, white with sugar. The sugar dispenser runs out of sugar after the first.

Now, document your design using the documentation style as top-view as in [Figure 12. Responsibilities are the shortest description of a unit's function] and with time-view diagrams.

3. The Coffee machine part 2.

After five machines are installed and have been operating for a while, Arnold comes along and says, "I would like to add bouillon, at twenty-five cents. Change the design."

We add one more button for bouillon, and one more container for bouillon powder. How else do you change your design?

Again, check the responsibilities, interactions, ***and your sensations*** about this little bureaucracy you are designing. Learn to feel your internal opinions about this little bureaucracy.

4. Coffee machine part 3.

Arnold comes back a while later with a brilliant idea. He has heard that some companies use their company badges to directly debit the cost of coffee purchases from the employees' paychecks. Since they already have badge readers, he thinks this should be a simple change.

We add a badge reader and link to payroll. I ask you to make the design change.

Ready, set, Go.

5. Coffee machine part 4.

People are wanting to buy lattes instead of his coffees. Arnold wants the machine modified just slightly, so that he can create a "drink of the week". He wants to be able to add new drinks and change prices anytime, to match his competition. He wants to be able to add espresso, cappuccino, hot chocolate, latte, choco-latte, steamed milk -- in short, anything he can mix together.

We add a couple more buttons, a milk steamer and dispenser, and a couple more powder dispensers. We conclude our cash box design is pretty safe, now, and discuss how to meet Arnold's request.

The first, and typical suggestion at this point, is to beef up the mainframe object so that it knows everything. I put my foot down, finally, and ask for a better, more robust design, so that we or Arnold can change the products and prices at will, without tearing the machine apart any further.

What do you come up with at this point? Ready, set, Go.

6. Media store part 1.

We're going to evolve the design of this little system over the next 3 exercises so you can see the pros and cons of more and fewer objects.

You've been asked to program up a little system for a small store that rents out items (you get to choose what they are renting, or leave it general). It will handle rentals and returns, but not do the financial accounting, that system already exists.

A customer would come in, find whatever it is they want, bring it to the cashier and rent it. Later, they return it and pay the rental fee. All the usual things about fees, penalties, damaged goods, exchanges, as usual.

In part 1, design the system with just TWO classes.

- What two did you choose, and why did you select those two?

7. Media store part 2.

In part 2, design the system with FIVE classes, no more, no less.

- Why did you choose those five?
- Do their names, responsibilities and signatures align?
- How you feel about this design compared with the design with just two classes?

5. Media store part 3.

In part 3, design the system with as many classes as you want, your choice of inheritance hierarchy.

- How do you feel about this design, compared with the one with just five classes?
- In what ways is this one better, and in what ways is the other better?
- For all of the object in your design, do their names, responsibilities and signatures align?

8. Checking account.

Make two designs for a normal checking account, with deposits, withdrawals, whatever you like.

In design 1, make deposit and withdrawal two of the subclasses.

In design 2, merge those classes , encode whether deposit or withdrawal in an instance variable instead of in the inheritance hierarchy.

Debate with a friend where things go, such as the override of a void on a check – is that a deposit or a withdrawal? What does it take to change the system when a new manager changes that decision?

9. Course certificates management part 1.

You are creating a system to track the use of courses to get advanced certificates. To make it more interesting, assume that it is for a consortium. The consortium publishes a spec for a course design, member companies get accredited for their course designs and given permission to teach their version of the course. Students take courses from various providers, getting a certificate for each course until they reach one of three levels (starter, intermediate, advanced).

How many classes do you need to make this work?

10. Course certificates management part 2.

Now simplify it. It's just your company, no others, you have a series of courses. There are no levels, just the courses. You have some accredited trainers. When one of them teaches, the certificate has to have both their and your signatures. When you teach, the certificate will only need your one signature. How few classes do you need to make this work well?

Answers and Discussion

Here are some answers to the exercises. These are my chosen ways to do things. Yours might look better to you. Consider complexity and ease of understanding as part of your looking.

1. Design an actual physical bank. How would you document it on just one page?

I ran this exercise for a while just to see how people describe things to each other, without constraints. What showed up was they wanted to see the interactions between the parts of the bank (think: parts, responsibilities and interactions), and since it's a bank, they wanted to know what services it offers.

It was from these exercises that I locked onto responsibilities and interactions as the dominant way to document a system.

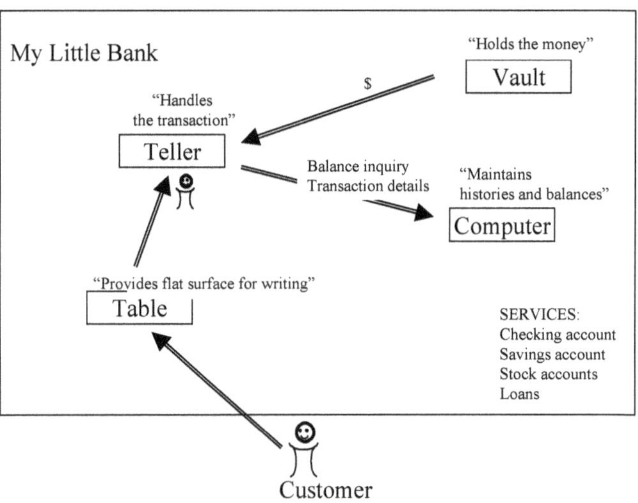

Figure 41, Appendix A. Documenting a small bank.

2. Coffee machine part 1.

What's fun about including these answers to this exercise is that I wrote these solutions years ago. Since then, various people have objected to various part of the design, to which I could only reply, "Um, yes, you're right." See where you find objections and where your design fixes or fails in comparison.

Here is the design I came up with:

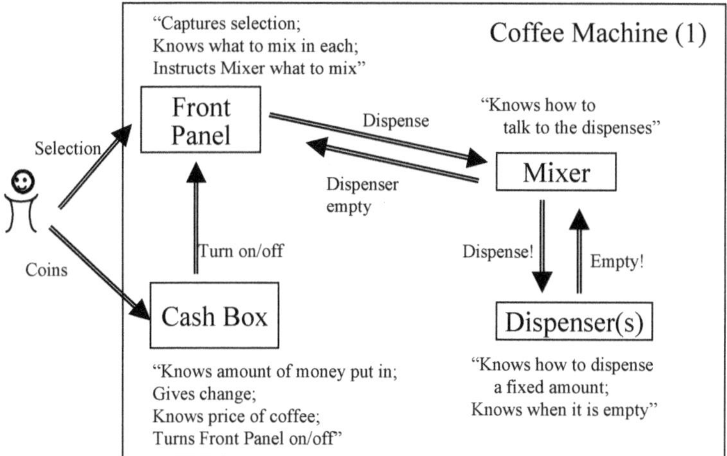

Figure 42, Appendix A. Coffee machine 1, responsibilities view.

This design has four main components:

Cash Box: Knows amount of money put in; Gives change; Knows price of coffee; Turns Front Panel on and off.

Front Panel: Captures selection; Knows what to mix in each; Instructs Mixer what to mix.

Mixer: Knows how to talk to the dispensers.

Dispensers (cup-, coffee powder-, sugar-, creamer-, water-): Knows how to dispense a fixed amount; Knows when it is empty.

Here are their interactions for running out of sugar:

Coffee Machine(1) in operation, running out of sugar

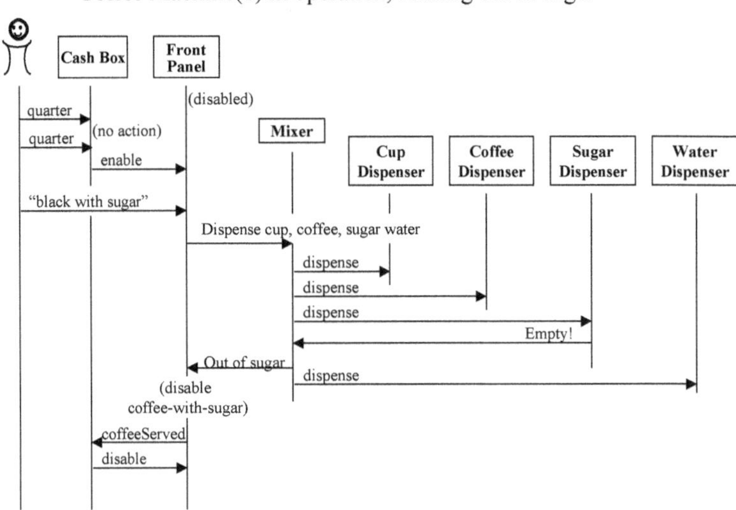

<u>Figure 43, Appendix A.</u> Coffee machine 1, time view.

There are some things that may look strange to you in this design, but that keep it to only four types of objects.

The first and perhaps most obvious is that the front panel knows what ingredients are needed in what order. My goal here was to have fewest objects, I couldn't justify adding another controller that knew the mapping from product to dispensers.

The second is that the cash box turns the front panel on and off. As the buyer adds money, the cash box, which knows the fact that 35 cents is needed, will enable any drink selection. This reduces any back-and-forth between the front panel and the cash box.

The third is the separation of the mixer from the front panel. I didn't want the front panel to know all the details of how to turn on a dispenser, that just doesn't seem like something a front panel should know. So the mixer is just that interface object that knows about dispensers.

Your mileage may vary, as they say. What I care about is that you practice feeling what it is like "owning" responsibilities. "Not my job"

/ "Shouldn't need to know" and "too much back-and-forth" being key reactions.

Reflection: The one place that I got caught out on with this design was the name "Front Panel." Did you also spot that? The person said, "That name not only doesn't say what it does, it only says where it is." To which I can only say, "Um, yes, you're right." What did you call it?

The other part to reflect on is that typically, designers create too many different objects, cluttering up the design and overloading the reader's mind. Given the requirements we have so far, there is no need for more objects ... those will come over time as requirements get added. If none get added, then we are done with this simple design.

3. Coffee machine part 2.

The addition of the bouillon at a different price changes what is appropriate to have the cash box know. Now there is a link between product and price which wasn't there before.

Originally, there was just one price, so the cash box could reasonably be asked to turn on the front panel when there was enough money. If we now have a link between product and price, we have split the knowledge of a product into two places, the cash box knows a product's price, while the front panel knows the product's ingredients. Don't like that.

Keeping the same objects, I shifted the knowledge of the product's price to the where the ingredients are, so they are together.

As a consequence, now the direction of the conversation changes: The front panel now has to ask the cash box, "Do you have 25 (or 35) cents?"

Here is the responsibility interaction diagram for this design.

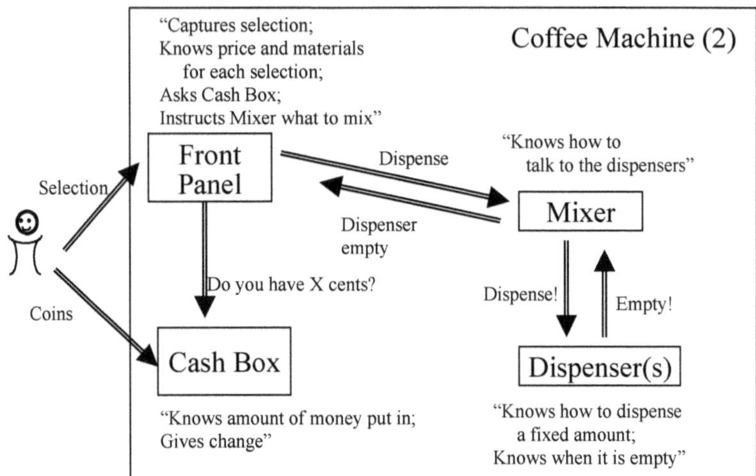

Figure 44, Appendix A. Coffee machine 2, responsibilities view.

Cash Box: Knows amount of money put in; Gives change.

Front Panel: Captures selection; Knows price of selections, materials needed for each; Asks Cash Box if enough money has been put in; Instructs Mixer what to mix.

Mixer: same as before.

Dispensers: same as before.

Here is the interaction diagram:

Coffee Machine(2) in operation

Figure 45, Appendix A. Coffee machine 2, time view.

Snap analysis of designs 1 and 2

Supposedly, we should design to reduce the impact of changes. Notice that we have completely revamped the machine. Ack. Evidently, the first design was, in hindsight, not such a robust design. The key error was that the cash box knew the price of the coffee. That means that asking for price by drink raises havoc with the design.

The new design is better in this regard. Since the front panel knows the selections and the price, we can change prices at will, and only change one component.

In discussion with my co-designer (or myself, if were alone), I voice a worry at this point: the front panel looks awfully smart. It hardly deserves to be called a "front panel".

I call this the "mainframe" approach to design. One of the objects in the system has all the smarts. Almost any change to the system can be accomplished by changing the mainframe object.

You may have come up with a slightly different mainframe approach. You keep the front panel dumb; all it does is register a selection. You add a fifth object, which in a spark of inspiration, you call the

Controller. The Controller knows everything the second design's front panel knows, only does not physically have the buttons. The front panel tells the Controller it the selection, the Controller talks to the cash box, the Controller tells the mixer what to dispense.

<u>One attraction of the mainframe approach is that the "trajectory of change" is only one object</u>. That sounds great, but what happens over time is that people keep adding more and more responsibilities to that one object until no one knows how to subdivide it any more, <u>no one will touch it to clean it up</u>. A typo in the mainframe object means damage to any of many modules, with endless testing and unpredictable bugs. Those readers who have done system maintenance or legacy system replacement will recognize that almost every large system ends up with such a module, and will affirm what sort of a nightmare it becomes.

Although I voice the worry, I cannot quantify it, and so we leave the design the way it is, with either the front panel or the controller being the baby mainframe object.

4. Coffee machine part 3.

You should find that this is not as bad as it sounds. To make the result clean and robust, we really only need a change in mindset.

Since no money was put in, it is no longer possible to ask the cash box for the amount of money put in. But we can borrow the inquiry used by major credit cards. When you go to pay for a meal, the restaurant does not ask American Express or Visa, "How much money does this person have?" (for security reasons). The restaurant asks, "Can this person accept a charge of the following amount?" The answer comes back yes or no.

So we just change the question to the cash box to: "Does the customer have <amount> credit?"

Now, we are indifferent to whether the customer pays by cash or direct debit. Further, payroll can shut the credit down at a certain point, should the employee be terminated or appears to be buying for everyone in the building.

If your original design already worked this way, give yourself extra credit points. Even though it would have cost nothing to have designed this way from the start, the design was not obvious at the start. You might have arrived at the design if you had enquired after how the design requirements might evolve in the future.

The responsibility, "knows how much money is put in", is sensitive to assumptions and to a technology. "Knows whether there is sufficient credit", works the same for cash, but is less specific about assumptions and technology. It is therefore more robust.

Design 3 changes very little from design 2. The new responsibilities are:

Cash Box: Accepts cash or charge. Answers whether a given amount of credit is available.

Front Panel: same as before, but only asks Cash Box if sufficient credit is available.

Mixer and **dispenser**: same as before.

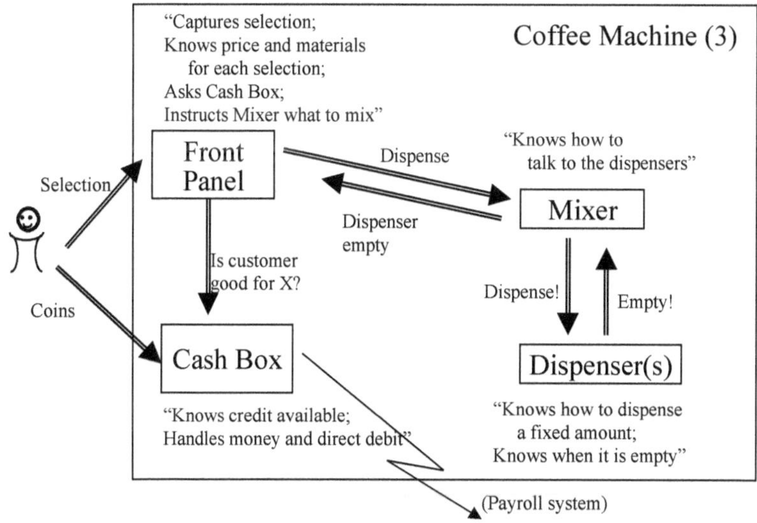

Figure 46, Appendix A. Coffee machine 3, responsibilities view.

Back in the heyday of C++, a colleague wrote some code for these desigs. The code is after we get done working through the story of Arnold and his friends. It is old code by today's standards, but still interesting in its construction

I am still not happy with the design. We'll see why, in the next part of the article. See if you can improve the design, and say why it is "better", while waiting.

5. Coffee machine part 4

The design we come up with at this point bears no resemblance to our original design. It is, I am happy to see, robust with respect to change, and it is a much more reasonable "model of the world". For the first time, we see *product* show up in the design. The responsibilities are evenly distributed. Each component has a single primary purpose in life; we have avoided piling responsibilities together. The names of the components match the responsibilities. And finally, we drop the name Front Panel and call it, more correctly, Product Selector.

Cash Box: Knows credit available. Handles money and direct debit.

Product Selector: Knows products, captures selection, coordinates Cash Box and Mixer to validate and produce the drink.

Product: Knows its own price and recipe.

Recipe: Knows the quantity and sequence of ingredients.

Ingredient: Knows what it is.

Mixer: Interprets a recipe, controls the dispensers.

Dispenser (cup-, coffee powder-, sugar-, creamer-, water-): Knows how to dispense a fixed amount; Knows when it is empty.

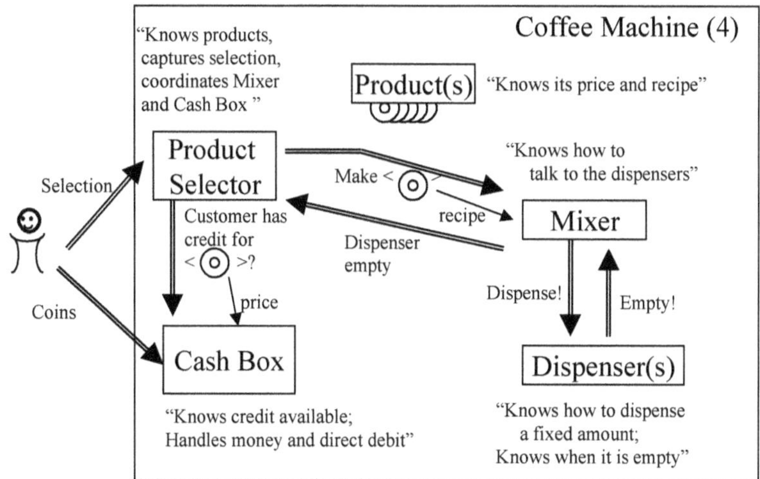

Figure 47, Appendix A. Coffee machine 4, responsibilities view.

When Arnold wants to add a product, we add a new Product to the existing set in the machine, and let the front panel know which button selects the new product. Should Arnold change the recipe or price of a product, we have exactly one, highly localized change to make. In other words, we have reduced the trajectory of change, as described in all the advertising on object technology.

For the first time, we have a component which is not static. The selected Product rolls around the system, sharing its knowledge with the fixed components. For many newcomers to OO, such an object is non-intuitive. It simplifies the machine considerably, and more importantly, it provides the localization of changes we have been searching for.

Coffee Machine (4) in operation

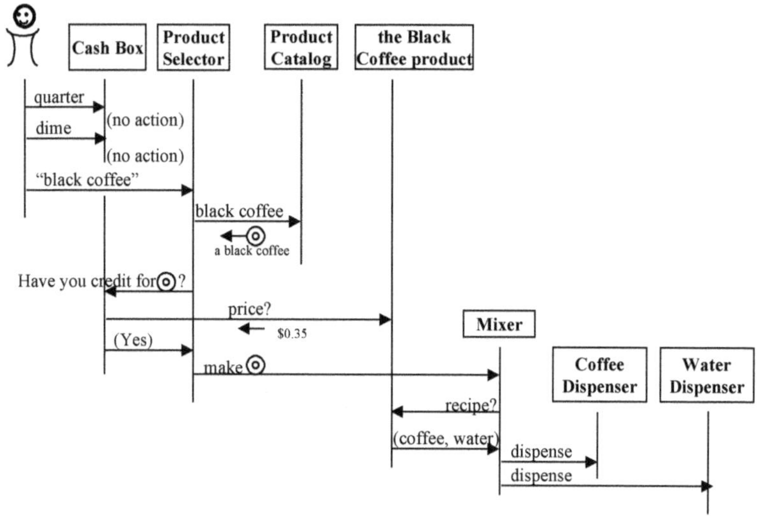

Figure 48, Appendix A. Coffee machine 4, time view.

5. Code for the coffee machine designs

In the interest of saving space in this little book, I don't include the code for these designs here. However, you can find some code and a longer discussion of the coffee machines online in the articles:

Coffee machine problem, part 1:
https://web.archive.org/web/20170606113834/http://alistair.cockburn.us/Coffee+machin e+design+problem%2c+part+1

and Coffee machine problem, part 2:
https://web.archive.org/web/20170608075902/http://alistair.cockburn.us/Coffee+machin e+design+problem%2c+part+2

8. Checking account.

The point I would like to make with this exercise is that subclasses and instance variables have a correspondence. You can solve the problem with either; what happens is that one is easier to change than the other. This was not obvious to me at the time, I learned it from handling this problem on a real project.

Our assignment is to make two designs for a normal checking account, with deposits, withdrawals, whatever you like.

In design 1, deposit and withdrawal are two of the subclasses.

In design 2, whether deposit or withdrawal is encoded in an instance variable instead of in the inheritance hierarchy.

Both designs work, the only difference comes with deciding were certain things go, such as the void on a deposit: Is that a negative deposit or a withdrawal? What does it take to change the system when a new manager changes that decision?

Below are two designs for you to consider. It turns out that the critical question is:

Do you model a void of a deposit as a deposit or as a withdrawal?

As you rush to answer that, I can tell you that I have found that the answer to this varies considerably with the person being asked, and there are many more than just two answers. I was not able even to understand some of the answers, so I cannot list them here. Try this out on your friends and colleagues, and see what they come up with.

The answer gets compounded when you go to display the result to the users – do they consider a void of a deposit as a deposit or a withdrawal? (And recall, almost any transaction can be voided, so this will apply to all transaction types, across the board.)

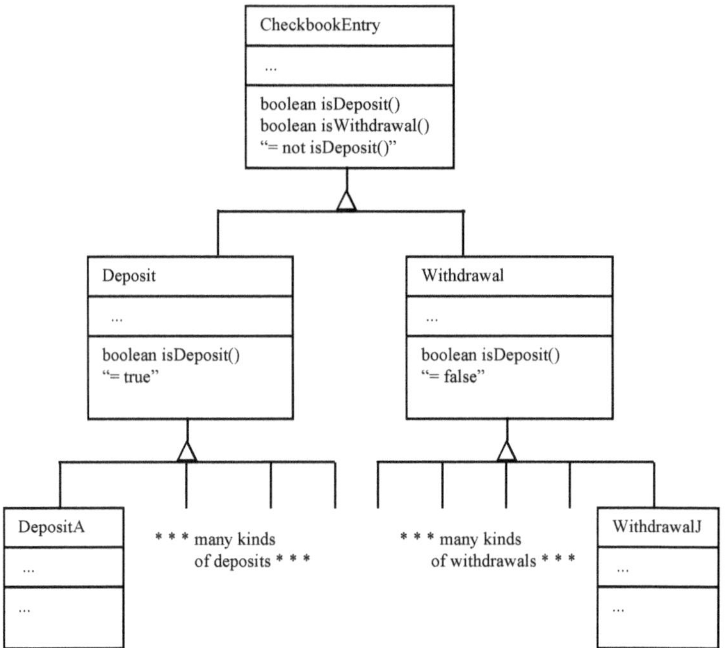

Figure 49, Appendix A. Deposits and withdrawals as subclasses

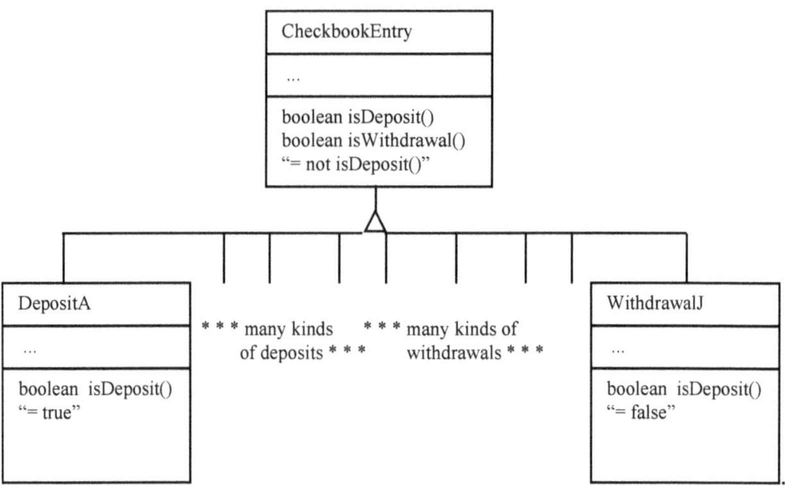

Figure 50, Appendix A. Deposit / withdrawal as a variable

Here is the discussion from the project where we ran into this:

There was no debate about this initial design. Everyone considered the model obvious and true.

Then we encountered the voids. Each week, as we interviewed more people, we got new and different answers to the question about a voided deposit, to the point that we felt we could not trust the stability of any answer.

It was, however, clear that the users wanted to see a voided deposit in the Deposits column.

We decided in the end that while we could trust that the two dozen kinds of checkbook entries would continue to exist, there was nothing intrinsic or stable about the classes Deposit and Withdrawal. Each entry had to be able to answer whether it was a deposit or withdrawal, and we were clearly going to change our minds quite often as to how a voided deposit would answer that question.

Eventually, we created about two dozen subclasses under the CheckbookEntry class, one for each entry type, including voided entry (see Figure 50). Rather than locking the answer to "Are you a deposit?" into the class hierarchy, we gave each entry type a method to answer whether it was a deposit or withdrawal. The reason for moving the question from the class structure to a method is that changing the class structure is a serious change to the system, while changing a method's answer from "true" to "false" is minor.

Once we created this design, we stopped worrying about the answer to the question, "is a voided deposit a deposit or a withdrawal?". That could change every week without holding up the project. To this day I do not know what the final answer came out to be, nor do I worry. The software design was adequate, timely, stable, efficient and a reasonable model of the business.

What I learned from this experience was that encoding information in the class hierarchy is equivalent in many ways to encoding it in an instance variable. They introduce different types of complexity.

- The class hierarchy answer allows sharing of inherited code, which simplifies extending the behaviors.

- The instance variable answer forces duplication of code, but allows the answer to the "voided deposit" question to change very easily.

My net takeaway from the experience was that I wished it could be a simple refactoring move to change from subclass to instance variable and back again, so that this decision wouldn't be a major but a minor one. We wasted way too much time on that project debating this question.

Appendix A: The 1972 Parnas paper on modularization

D.L. Parnas wrote what I consider the foundational article on designing to reduce the trajectory of change. Whenever I am wondering how much we have advanced over the last 50 years, or need to double-check my assumptions and my language, I go back and re-read this paper.

Don't dismiss the paper because he uses what we today consider a trivial problem. Pay attention to the way he presents his line of thinking. Also, don't pay attention to his other paper, in which he talks about "information hiding." As he makes clear in the conclusion, it's not the *information* we are trying to corral and protect, it's the *decisions* that we are gathering into one place.

Here is the key sentence from the conclusion.

> *"one begins with a list of difficult design decisions or design decisions which are likely to change. Each module is then designed to hide such a decision from the others."*

I feel like all our work in the 1990s and since has been just to find language and techniques to do what he says.

You can find a PDF of the paper online, for instance: [https://wstomv.win.tue.nl/edu/2ip30/references/criteria_for_modularization.pdf]

D.L. Parnas *On the Criteria To Be Used in Decomposing Systems into Modules*

Reprinted from *Communications of the ACM*, Vol. 15, No. 12, December 1972 pp. 1053 - 1058 Copyright © 1972, Association for Computing Machinery Inc.

This paper discusses modularization as a mechanism for improving the flexibility and comprehensibility of a system while allowing the shortening of its development time. The effectiveness of a "modularization" is dependent upon the criteria used in dividing the system into modules. A system design problem is presented and both a conventional and unconventional decomposition are described. It is shown that the unconventional decompositions have distinct advantages for the goals outlined. The criteria used in arriving at the decompositions are discussed. The unconventional decomposition, if implemented with the conventional assumption that a module consists of one or more subroutines, will be less efficient in most cases. An alternative approach to implementation which does not have this effect is sketched.

Key Words and Phrases: software, modules, modularity, software engineering, KWIC index, software design

CR Categories: 4.0

Introduction

A lucid statement of the philosophy of modular programming can be found in a 1970 textbook on the design of system programs by Gouthier and Pont [1,10.23], which we quote below:

A well-defined segmentation of the project effort ensures system modularity. Each task forms a separate, distinct program module. At implementation time each module and its inputs and outputs are well-defined, there is no confusion in the intended interface with other system modules. At checkout time the integrity of the module is tested independently; there are few scheduling problems in synchronizing the completion of several tasks before checkout can begin. Finally, the system is maintained in modular fashion, system errors and deficiencies can be traced to specific system modules, thus limiting the scope of detailed error searching.

Usually nothing is said about the criteria to be used in dividing the system into modules. This paper will discuss that issue and, by means of examples, suggest some criteria which can be used in decomposing a system into modules.

A Brief Status Report

The major advancement in the area of modular programming has been the development of coding techniques and assemblers which (1) allow one module to be written with little knowledge of the code in another module, and (2) allow modules to be reassembled and replaced without reassembly of the whole system. This facility is extremely valuable for the production of large pieces of code, but the systems most often used as examples of problem systems are highly modularized programs and make use of the techniques mentioned above.

Expected Benefits of Modular Programming

The benefits expected of modular programming are:

(1) managerial – development time should be shortened because separate groups would work on each module with little need for communication:

(2) product flexibility – it should be possible to make drastic changes to one module without a need to change others;

(3) comprehensibility – it should be possible to study the system one module at a time. The whole system can therefore be better designed because it is better understood.

What Is Modularization?

Below are several partial system descriptions called *modularizations*. In this context "module" is considered to be a responsibility assignment rather than a subprogram. The *modularizations* include the design decisions which must be made *before* the work on independent modules can begin. Quite different decisions are included for each alternative, but in all cases the intention is to describe all "system level" decisions (i.e. decisions which affect more than one module).

Example System 1: A KWIC Index Production System

The following description of a KWIC index will suffice for this paper. The KWIC index system accepts an ordered set of lines, each line is an ordered set of words, and each word is an ordered set of characters. Any line may be "circularly shifted" by repeatedly removing the first word and appending it at the end of the line. The KWIC index system outputs a listing of all circular shifts of all lines in alphabetical order.

This is a small system. Except under extreme circumstances (huge data base, no supporting software), such a system could be produced by a good programmer within a week or two. Consequently, none of the difficulties motivating modular programming are important for this system. Because it is impractical to treat a large system thoroughly, we must go through the exercise of treating this problem as if it were a large project. We give one modularization which typifies current approaches, and another which has been used successfully in undergraduate class projects.

Modularization 1

We see the following modules:

Module 1: Input. This module reads the data lines from the input medium and stores them in core for processing by the remaining modules. The characters are packed four to a word, and an otherwise unused character is used to indicate the end of a word. An index is kept to show the starting address of each line.

Module 2: Circular Shift. This module is called after the input module has completed its work. It prepares an index which gives the address of the first character of each circular shift, and the original index of the line in the array made up by module 1. It leaves its output in core with words in pairs (original line number, starting address).

Module 3: Alphabetizing. This module takes as input the arrays produced by modules I and 2. It produces an array in the same format as that produced by module 2. In this case, however, the circular shifts are listed in another order (alphabetically).

Module 4: Output. Using the arrays produced by module 3 and module 1, this module produces a nicely formatted output listing all of the circular shifts. In a sophisticated system the actual start of each line will be marked, pointers to further information may be inserted, and the start of the circular shift may actually not be the first word in the line, etc.

Module 5: Master Control. This module does little more than control the sequencing among the other four modules. It may also handle error messages, space allocation, etc.

It should be clear that the above does not constitute a definitive document. Much more information would have to be supplied before work could start. The defining documents would include a number of pictures showing core formats, pointer conventions, calling conventions, etc. All of the interfaces between the four modules must be specified before work could begin.

This is a modularization in the sense meant by all proponents of modular programming. The system is divided into a number of modules with well-defined interfaces; each one is small enough and simple enough to be thoroughly understood and well programmed. Experiments on a small scale indicate that this is approximately the decomposition which would be proposed by most programmers for the task specified.

Modularization 2

We see the following modules:

Module 1: Line Storage. This module consists of a number of functions or subroutines which provide the means by which the user of the module may call on it. The function call *CHAR(r,w,c)* will have as value an integer representing the cth character in the rth line, wth word. A call such as *SETCHAR(rpv,c,d)* will cause the cth character in the wth word of the rth line to be the character represented by d (i.e. *CHAR(r,w,c) = d*). *WORDS(r)* returns as value the number of words in line *r*. There are certain restrictions in the way that these routines may be called; if these restrictions are violated the routines "trap" to an error-handling subroutine which is to be provided by the users of the routine. Additional routines are available which reveal to the caller the number of words in any line, the number of lines currently stored, and the number of characters in any word. Functions *DELINE* and *DELWRD* are provided to delete portions of lines which have already been stored. A precise specification of a similar module has been given in [3] and [8] and we will not repeat it here.

Module 2: INPUT. This module reads the original lines from the input media and calls the line storage module to have them stored internally.

Module 3: Circular Shifter. The principal functions provided by this module are analogs of functions provided in module 1. The module creates the impression that we have created a line holder containing not all of the lines but all of the circular shifts of the lines. Thus the function call *CSCHAR(I,w,c)* provides the value representing the cth character in the wth word of the Ith circular shift. It is specified that (1) if $i < j$ then the shifts of line i precede the shifts of line j, and (2) for each line the first shift is the original line, the second shift is obtained by making a one-word rotation to the first shift, etc. A function *CSSETUP* is provided which must be called before the other functions have their specified values. For a more precise specification of such a module see [8].

Module 4: Alphabetizer. This module consists principally of two functions. One, *ALPH,* must be called before the other will have a defined value. The second, *ITH,* will serve as an index. *ITH(i)* will give the index of the circular shift which comes ith in the alphabetical ordering. Formal definitions of these functions are given [8].

Module 5: Output. This module will give the desired printing of set of lines or circular shifts.

Module 6: Master Control. Similar in function to the modularization above.

Comparison of the Two Modularizations

General. Both schemes will work. The first is quite conventional; the second has been used successfully in a class project [7]. Both will reduce the programming to the relatively independent programming of a number of small, manageable, programs.

Note first that the two decompositions may share all data representations and access methods. Our discussion is about two different ways of cutting up what *may* be the same object. A system built according to decomposition I could conceivably be identical *after assembly* to one built according to decomposition 2. The differences between the two alternatives are in the way that they are divided into the work assignments, and the interfaces between modules. The algorithms used in both cases *might* be identical. The systems are substantially different even if identical in the runnable representation. This is possible because the runnable representation need only be used for running; other representations are used for changing, documenting, understanding, etc. The two systems will not be identical in those other representations.

Changeability. There are a number of design decisions which are questionable and likely to change under many circumstances. This is a partial list.

1. Input format.

2. The decision to have all lines stored in core. For large jobs it may prove inconvenient or impractical to keep all of the lines in core at any one time.

3. The decision to pack the characters four to a word. In cases where we are working with small amounts of data it may prove undesirable to pack the characters; time will be saved by a character per word layout. In other cases we may pack, but in different formats.

4. The decision to make an index for the circular shifts rather that actually store them as such. Again, for a small index or a large core, writing them out may be the preferable approach. Alternatively, we may choose to prepare nothing during *CSSETUP* All computation could be done during the calls on the other functions such as *CSCHAR*.

5. The decision to alphabetize the list once, rather than either (a) search for each item when needed, or (b) partially alphabetize as is done in Hoare's FIND [2]. In a number of circumstances it would be advantageous to distribute the computation involved in alphabetization over the time required to produce the index.

By looking at these changes we can see the differences between the two modularizations. The first change is confined to one module in both decompositions. For the first decomposition the second change would result in changes in every module! The same is true of the third change. In the first decomposition the format of the line storage in core must be used by all of the programs. In the second decomposition the story is entirely different. Knowledge of the exact way that the lines are stored is entirely hidden from all but module 1. Any change in the manner of storage can be confined to that module!

In some versions of this system there was an additional module in the decomposition. A symbol table module (as specified in [3]) was used within the line storage module. This fact was completely invisible to the rest of the system.

The fourth change is confined to the circular shift module in the second decomposition, but in the first decomposition the alphabetizer and the output routines will also know of the change.

The fifth change will also prove difficult in the first decomposition. The output module will expect the index to have been completed before it began. The alphabetizer module in the second decomposition was designed so that a user could not detect when the alphabetization was actually done. No other module need be changed.

Independent Development. In the first modularization the interfaces between the modules are the fairly complex formats and table organizations described above. These represent design decisions which cannot be taken lightly. The table structure and organization are essential to the efficiency of the various modules and must be designed carefully. The development of those formats will be a major part of the module development and that part must be a joint effort among the several development groups. In the second modularization the interfaces are more abstract; they consist primarily in the function names and the numbers and types of the parameters. These are relatively simple decisions and the independent development of modules should begin much earlier.

Comprehensibility. To understand the output module in the first modularization, it will be necessary to understand something of the alphabetizer, the circular shifter, and the input module. There will be aspects of the tables used by output which will only make sense because of the way that the other modules work. There will be constraints on the structure of the tables due to the algorithms used in the other modules. The system will only be comprehensible as a whole.

It is my subjective judgment that this is not true in the second modularization.

The Criteria

Many readers will now see what criteria were used in each decomposition. In the first decomposition the criterion used was to make each major step in the processing a module. One might say that to get the first decomposition one makes a flowchart. This is the most common approach to decomposition or modularization. It is an outgrowth of all programmer training which teaches us that we should begin with a rough flowchart and move from there to a detailed implementation. The flowchart was a useful abstraction for systems with on the order of 5,000-10,000 instructions, but as we move beyond that it does not appear to be sufficient; something additional is needed.

The second decomposition was made using "information hiding" [41 as a criterion. The modules no longer correspond to steps in the processing. The line storage module, for example, is used in almost every action by the system. Alphabetization may or may not correspond to a phase in the processing according to the method used. Similarly, circular shift might, in some circumstances, not make any table at all but calculate each character as demanded. Every module in the second decomposition is characterized by its knowledge of a design decision which it hides from all others. Its interface or definition was chosen to reveal as little as possible about its inner workings.

Improvement in Circular Shift Module

To illustrate the impact of such a criterion let us take a closer look at the design of the circular shift module from the second decomposition. Hindsight now suggests that this definition reveals more information than necessary. While we carefully hid the method of storing or calculating the list of circular shifts, we specified an order to that list. Programs could be effectively written if we specified only (I) that the lines indicated in circular shift's current definition will all exist in the table, (2) that no one of them would be included twice, and (3) that an additional function existed which would allow us to identify the original line given the shift. By prescribing the order for the shifts we have given more information than necessary and so unnecessarily restricted the class of systems that we can build without changing the definitions. For example, we have not allowed for a system in which the circular shifts were produced in alphabetical order, *ALPH is* empty, and *ITH* simply returns its argument as a value. Our failure to do this in constructing the systems with the second decomposition must clearly be classified as a design error.

In addition to the general criteria that each module hides some design decision from the rest of the system, we can mention some specific examples of decompositions which seem advisable.

1. A *data structure*, its internal linkings, *accessing procedures and modifying procedures* are part of a single module. They are not shared by many modules as is conventionally done. This notion is perhaps just an elaboration of the assumptions behind the papers of Balzer [9] and Mealy [10]. Design with this in mind is clearly behind the design of BLISS [11].

2. *The sequence of instructions necessary to call a given routine and the routine itself are part of the same module.* This rule was not relevant in the Fortran systems used for experimentation but it becomes essential for systems constructed in an assembly language. There are no perfect general calling sequences for real machines and consequently they tend to vary as we continue our search for the ideal sequence. By assigning responsibility for generating the call to the person responsible for the routine we make such improvements easier and also make it more feasible to have several distinct sequences in the same software structure.

3. The *formats of control blocks* used in queues in operating systems and similar programs *must be hidden* within a "control block module." It is

conventional to make such formats the interfaces between various modules. Because design evolution forces frequent changes on control block formats such a decision often proves extremely costly.

4. *Character codes, alphabetic orderings and similar data should be hidden* in a module for greatest flexibility. 5. The sequence in which certain items `will` be processed should (as far as practical) be hidden within a single module. Various changes ranging from equipment additions to unavailability of certain resources in an operating system make sequencing extremely variable.

Efficiency and Implementation

If we are not careful the second decomposition will prove to be much less efficient than the first. If each of the functions is actually implemented as a procedure with an elaborate calling sequence there will be a great deal of such calling due to the repeated switching between modules. The first decomposition will not suffer from this problem because there is relatively infrequent transfer of control between modules.

To save the procedure call overhead, yet gain the advantages that we have seen above, we must implement these modules in an unusual way. In many cases the routines will be best inserted into the code by an assembler; in other cases, highly specialized and efficient transfers would be inserted. To successfully and efficiently make use of the second type of decomposition will require a tool by means of which programs may be written as if the functions were subroutines, but assembled by whatever implementation is appropriate. If such a technique is used, the separation between modules may not be clear in the final code. For that reason additional program modification features would also be useful. In other words, the several representations of the program (which were mentioned earlier) must be maintained in the machine together with a program performing mapping between them.

A Decomposition Common to a Compiler and Interpretor for the Same Language

In an earlier attempt to apply these decomposition rules to a design project we constructed a translator for a Markov algorithm expressed in the notation described in [6]. Although it was not our intention to investigate the relation between compiling and interpretive translators of a language, we discovered that our decomposition was valid for a pure compiler and several varieties of interpreters for the language. Although there would be deep and substantial differences in the final running representations of each type of compiler, we found that the decisions implicit in the early decomposition held for all.

This would not have been true if we had divided responsibilities along the classical lines for either a compiler or interpretor (e.g. syntax recognizer, code generator, run time routines for a compiler). Instead the decomposition was based upon the hiding of various decisions as in the example above. Thus register representation, search algorithm, rule interpretation etc. were modules and these problems existed in both compiling and interpretive translators. Not only was the decomposition valid in all cases, but many of the routines could be used with only slight changes in any sort of translator.

This example provides additional support for the statement that the order in time in which processing is expected to take place should not be used in making the decomposition into modules. It further provides evidence that a careful job of decomposition can result in considerable carryover of work from one project to another.

A more detailed discussion of this example was contained in [8].

Hierarchical Structure

We can find a program hierarchy in the sense illustrated by Dijkstra [5] in the system defined according to decomposition 2. If a symbol table exists, it functions without any of the other modules, hence it is on level 1. Line storage is on level I if no symbol table is used or it is on level 2 otherwise. Input and Circular Shifter require line storage for their functioning. Output and Alphabetizer will require Circular Shifter, but since Circular Shifter and line holder are in some sense compatible, it would be easy to build a parameterized version of those routines which could be used to alphabetize or print out either the original lines or the circular shifts. In the first usage they would not require Circular Shifter; in the second they would. In other words, our design has allowed us to have a single representation for programs which may run at either of two levels in the hierarchy.

In discussions of system structure it is easy to confuse the benefits of a good decomposition with those of a hierarchical structure. We have a hierarchical structure if a certain relation may be defined between the modules or programs and that relation is a partial ordering. The relation we are concerned with is "uses" or "depends upon." It is better to use a relation between programs since in many cases one module depends upon only part of another module (e.g. Circular Shifter depends only on the output parts of the line holder and not on the correct working of *SKI WORD*). It is conceivable that we could obtain the benefits that we have been discussing without such a partial ordering, e.g. if all the modules were on the same level. The partial ordering gives us two additional benefits. First, parts of the system are benefited (simplified) because they use the services of lower levels. Second, we are able to cut off the upper levels and still have a usable and useful product. For example, the symbol table can be used in other applications; the line holder could be the basis of a question answering system. The existence of the hierarchical structure assures us that we can "prune" off the upper levels of the tree and start a new tree on the old trunk. If we had designed a system in which the "low level" modules made some use of the "high level" modules, we would not have the hierarchy, we would find it much harder to remove portions of the system, and "level" would not have much meaning in the system.

Since it is conceivable that we could have a system with the type of decomposition shown in version I (important design decisions in the interfaces) but retaining a hierarchical structure, we must conclude that hierarchical structure and "clean" decomposition are two desirable but *independent* properties of a system structure.

Conclusion

We have tried to demonstrate by these examples that it is almost always incorrect to begin the decomposition of a system into modules on the basis of a flowchart. We propose instead that one begins with a list of difficult design decisions or design decisions which are likely to change. Each module is then designed to hide such a decision from the others. Since, in most cases, design decisions transcend time of execution, modules will not correspond to steps in the processing. To achieve an efficient implementation we must abandon the assumption that a module is one or more subroutines, and instead allow subroutines and programs to be assembled collections of code from various modules.

Received August 1971; revised November 1971

References

I. Gauthier, Richard, and Pont, Stephen. *Designing Systems Programs, (C),* Prentice-Hall, Englewood Cliffs, N.J., 1970.

2. Hoare, C. A. R. Proof of a program, FIND. *Comm. ACM 14* 1 (Jan. 1971), 39-45.

3. Parnas, D. L. A technique for software module specification with examples. *Comm. ACM 15,* 5 (May, 1972), 330-336.

4. Parnas, D. L. Information distribution aspects of design methodology. Tech. Rept., Depart. Computer Science, Carnegie Mellon U., Pittsburgh, Pa., 1971. Also presented at the IFIP Congress 1971, Ljubljana, Yugoslavia.

5. Dijkstra, E. W. The structure of "THE"-multiprogramming system. *Comm. ACM 11,* 5 (May 1968), 341-346.

6. Galler, B., and Perlis, A. J. *A View of* Programming *Languages,* Addison-Wesley, Reading, Mass., 1970.

7. Parnas, D. L. A course on software engineering. Proc. SIGCSE Technical Symposium, Mar. 1972.

8. Parnas, D. L. On the criteria to be used in decomposing systems into modules. Tech. Rept., Depart.. Computer Science, Carnegie-Mellon U., Pittsburgh, Pa., 1971.

9. Balzer, R. M. Dataless programming. Proc. AFIPS 1967 FJCC, Vol. 31, AFIPS Press, Montvale, N.J., pp. 535-544.

10. Mealy, G. H. Another look at data. Proc. AFIPS 1967 FJCC Vol. 31, AFIPS Press, Montvale, N.J., pp. 525-534.

11. Wulf, W. A., Russell, D. B., and Habermann, A. N. BLISS A language for systems programming *Comm. ACM 14,* 12 (Dec. 1971), 780-790.

MAC / 1996-May-4

Appendix B: The Responsibility-Based Modeling Guides

The following are instruction guides I wrote in the mid 1990s for either or both of modeling a business or designing software using responsibilities as the modeling technique.

At that time, I had not yet narrowed down the two questions core to bureaucracy design, but you can see them lying in wait.

There is some repetition across the guides, but also some different nuances in each, as each was written for a different audience. See which one has the details you need.

B.1. *"Setting up for CRC Card Exercises"*

A CRC card is an informal work space intended to capture rapidly changing information. Different sizes may be used as available (common sizes are 3"x5" and 4"x6", with advocates for each). The card describes the information used by instance of the component. In the responsibility-based modeling activity, the card is treated as an instance. Should it become necessary to create a card describing the class as an object itself, have the name on the card end in the word "class" (e.g., Checking Accounts class).

The component name is written across the top. The responsibilities are written in three groups.

First is a brief summary, or synopsis, of the responsibilities of the component, its role in the system. This should be a short phrase, or perhaps two (see example).

Next, in a list down the left side of the card are the active responsibilities, with a line or arrow to the right, ending in the name of a required collaborator for that responsibility. An active responsibility starts with an active verb, such as "track", "compute" or "find". Avoid the word "manage" where possible, and the passive verb, "hold".

Last are the contact point responsibilities, the information the component mediates. Often these will come from the attributes in a data or business model. If there is some question whether a service belongs in the active or contact point responsibility section, choose arbitrarily with a slight inclination toward the the contact point section. It really does not matter a great deal. In the end, all responsibilities will be treated equally. The purpose in having the sections is so that attention can be focused on the summary and active responsibilities, which are the primary vehicle for partitioning the system. The contact point responsibilities are needed for component specification, and to demonstrate how the components deliver the required function in a documented scenario.

1 - Set up the activity.

Use a centrally visible and accessible table.

Have available a stack of blank CRC cards (see. Place them on the table within reach of anyone or give everyone a set for themselves.

Ideally 2-4 people. CRC works best when there is a discussion partner. More than 4 people results in people sitting idle and bored or diverting the discussion.

Walk through and role play a scenario, inventing and identifying components and responsibilities. Start by stating the message and information that starts the scenario, and the intended outcome. Pretend the design participants are the individual components, and have to deliver the function in the way the scenario says. The people role play the components.

On feeling embarrassed. It feels odd to begin with, pretending to be a component and not knowing what the component should do. Although it may feel odd, it is by pretending to be the component that a person can best address whether a responsibility is correct or not.

Ask what kind of component should handle the entry. Pick up the card for that component. Hypothesize the responsibility and the component, inventing new ones if necessary.

Note: Here is your big opportunity for reuse. Use things that exist, if possible.

Identify what the component would need to get its job done. Look into the catalog of existing components for a component that already does it. If none does, carry on asking what kind of component should have the needed responsibility.

Continue in this way until the scenario reaches its conclusion, using the responsibility-based modeling technique.

Tip: When things get moving rapidly, sometimes there is no time to write down the name of the responsibility or the name of the component. At those times, just point to an existing card or even to a blank spot on the table, either naming the component or just saying, "this one". If the design works, the component will show up consistently, and a good name can be discovered for it and its responsibilities. A good name is so important that it is worth delaying the naming of a component until its purpose is clear and agreed upon.

Tip: Pay attention to the level of the discussion. As mentioned above, it is fine to go deeper than the level of the design session periodically. The components nominated at other levels may become elements of subsystems that will eventually be designed. Note the components that belong to a different level, and either stack them under the card that is calling for their use, or set them to the side, so that they can be pointed to or reintroduced when there is a question.

Tip: Only use one pen. That way, it does not happen that one person changes the name, responsibilities or collaborators without the rest of the team noticing. The pen acts as a synchronization mechanism for the group.

The role play is an act of creation, in which design points are discovered, components and responsibilities are nominated, and design decisions are made. A choice between two names, between the need for a component or not, between two places to allocate a responsibility, is made is made by comparing the two choices against a set of scenarios. That choice is preferred which responds best to the scenarios. The choice is made on the basis of:

- (1) the responsibilities allocate in a more natural way,
- (2) the communication pattern between components is simpler,
- (3) the locus of change for varied assumptions is smaller.
- (4) (Occasionally, there appears no discernible difference between two choices. In this case, just choose one and proceed. See "Common Situations", below.)

It is therefore often appropriate in making a well-considered decision, to interrupt a scenario on occasion and explore some variations. The variations may try alternative assumptions about future requirements or implementations, or of usage.

2 - Manage the cards.

Typically, name a card immediately, but no great need to.

Sometimes people want to nominate a component. Fine. Put the card on the table. Ask what its responsibility is. If there appears to be a responsibility, write it down, either as an active responsibility or as a contact point. Let the card survive on its own merits.

Sometimes people can tell that a card needs to be there, but do not know what its name or exact function is. Fine. Put a blank card there. Let its personality grow over time until its name and responsibilities become clear. Often the responsibilities will become clear first, and from the responsibilities a name will be formed.

Sometimes a card is named, but its responsibilities evolve to a point where the name no longer matches. Draw a line through the old name and write the new. Or, get a new card, put the new name and the responsibilities on it. Put the old card to the side.

Collapse cards for subsystems out of scope.

Frequently, the discussion goes to a different level of design. Cards are created that do not apply to the current level of design, but are useful for demonstrating the consequences of a design choice or for showing how a component would likely carry out its responsibilities. Rather than let the cards clutter up the table and the discussion, collect the cards that help implement a responsibility. Place them behind the component they help that is at the correct level of discussion. Then they can be brought out for examination when they are needed, and kept out of sight otherwise.

Similarly for generic components and variants. Occasionally, the discussion will center around the generic component. The variants will be of minor importance, but are present to establish their presence. Place the variants under the generic component, so the generic component can carry the conversation.. The variants can be brought out again as they are needed.

Ways to collect and arrange the components:

- By level of implementation. That is what has been discussed so far.

- By privacy. Arrange the components differently if they can be publicly known at this level of discussion, or if they are private in some way. Chances are the private components are at a different level.

- By lifetime. Look for components that are significantly shorter or longer lived than others. Consider whether they belong at the same level. Collecting the components by their lifetimes occasionally reveals something of interest about the system, the components, or their communications.

Let unused cards drift out.

Of the many cards that get nominated, some do not survive through the design session. If it appears that one or more cards are not likely to see action, they may be allowed to drift to the side or back of the working area. If they develop an importance, they can be brought back into play.

At the end of the session, if there are cards that were nominated but not used, bring them forward again for review. It should be clear that they did not manage to keep any responsibilities and so will not reach implementation. If there is disagreement on this, the person wanting to keep them must find a scenario in which they carry responsibilities.

Use interaction diagrams with or even instead of cards.

A design group comfortable interaction diagrams may decide to let the interaction diagram carry the discussion instead of the CRC cards. This is a matter of personal preference, since some people need to see the message flows to visualize the interactions. The time view form of the interaction diagrams carries exploratory discussion better than the top view. CRC cards still offer greater flexibility and mobility in an active design session.

If interaction diagrams are used instead of cards, write the key responsibility of each component by it on the diagram.

At a design review, the interaction diagrams are already available as a result of the design session. The interaction diagrams may be used to illustrate how responsibilities are passed along and invoked. A listing of the responsibilities of the components must be available during the review, either as a list, or on the CRC cards, or as annotations on the interaction diagrams.

At this point you should have a stack of cards with responsibilities, and a stack of interaction diagrams showing how the components deliver the scenarios.

3 - Consolidate components by level.

Identify the components that are appropriate for the level of design declared at the beginning of the design session.

The design of the system will be presented to readers at different levels. To simplify the understanding of the design, and to isolate changes in the future, the design of the system should be documented at a consistent level. Subsystems or components that carry out the responsibilities on behalf of a component on the declared level are to be collected separately and not used in the discussion of the system at the declared level.

For a business application, the first level should consist only of those components meaningful to a business person concerned with verifying that the workings of the system are consistent with the workings of the business. Each scenario must have a complete description and fully connected walkthrough using only the components at this level. A connected walkthrough is one in which all the responsibilities and needed information are visibly available using the selected components.

At any subsequent level, the scenarios for a subsystem must have a complete description and fully connected walkthrough using only the components that are appropriate for the declared level. It is up to the design team to evaluate which components are appropriate for the level and which belong to the implementation of a component at the declared level.

The intuition, business knowledge and common sense of the design team is the guide for what belongs at a level.

Collect separately the components and subsystems at deeper levels.

Keep the cards for later use.

The components outside the scope of the design are still useful. Probably, one of the design team members will be involved in the design of the subsystem using those deeper components, and will be able to use those cards to start the design.

It is not necessary to document the use of the components at a deeper level. Someone in the room may want to document their use to help with future design or future reference.

B.2. "A short guide with steps for CRC cards"

This guide was based on the courses I attended and taught from 1990-1994, and also from watching Ward Cunningham use the cards himself in one of his client visits. The resulting description is, of course, my take on all that.

What it is

CRC stands for "Class-Responsibility-Collaborator". It names a brainstorming technique that works with scenario walkthroughs to stress-test a design. It also supports a rapid and thorough exploration of design alternatives. It may be used during initial model construction as a brainstorming technique, and again later to evaluate the design. It may be done by one person, or up to 5 people, after which it needs careful facilitation.

In a CRC exercise, a card or piece of paper is made to represent an instance of an object type. Its responsibility is identified, either by invention or writing it from the object type definition. A use case scenario is begun. Someone talks through the scenario, and one or more people show the objects that work together to deliver the scenario. When one object uses another, the second object is said to be the first object's collaborator. The names, the responsibilities, and the collaborations summarize the design at a low but accurate level of precision.

Relationships to other techniques

Responsibility-driven modeling may be done with CRC cards, or from an object interaction diagram, or from an object type diagram. CRC sessions are more fluid and support faster design evolution, but are more prone to confusion. Working from object interaction diagrams is slower and serializes discussion, which can be useful to check a design or to pace the discussion in a group. Working from object type diagrams is mostly useful for testing a design.

Steps

Refer to longer guides for a more thorough description of working with CRC cards. This section is a summary.

Step 1. Decide to use CRC cards and choose an coherent set of use cases

- Decide to work with CRC cards as opposed to or in conjunction with object interaction diagrams and object type diagrams.

- Select a set of use cases which look as though they will touch a related set of object types. These provide the scenarios for the group to walk through.

Step 2. Put a card on the table

- Put a card onto the table for each object instance. This is the card for the external actor who triggers the use case.

- Put a second card on the table. This is the card to whom the first card will send its initial message.

Alternatively, put cards onto the table for all the known, relevant object types, and label the cards with their main responsibilities.

Step 3. Walk through the scenario, naming cards and responsibilities

- Walk through the handling of a scenario case pointing to or picking up the cards, naming their responsibilities and how they handle and delegate each request.

- In a brainstorming session, add new cards as new functions are needed, or reallocate the responsibilities of the cards already on the table. It is not always necessary to name both the object type and the responsibility at the moment the card is put onto the table, as long as they are both written before the end.

Step 4. Vary the situations, to stress test the cards

- At any time during the walkthrough, you may vary the assumptions on the use case, to see if that causes a shift in the handling. With a good design, the handling is the same, but with the addition of a future object, or the change to at most one card.

- If it is decided a new object is needed to create a more stable design, add a new card, with the needed responsibility put onto it.

- Not all the cards on the table need be used; some may drift out to the sides if they are not used much. The cards that are needed at the end are those that get put into the design.

Step 5. Add cards, push cards to the side, to let the design evolve

- CRC cards permit several design alternatives to sit on the table at the same time. An unpopular initial design may turn out to be a popular later design, or perhaps the final design is a small alteration of an initially rejected design.

- Do not throw cards away, but push them to the side, in case it turns out later they are useful.

Step 6. Write down the key responsibility decisions and interactions

- Often, the design turns around a few key decisions about the allocation of responsibilities. Write these down.

- It is not useful to draw interaction diagrams for all the scenarios considered, but it is very useful to draw a representative few.

Often, while one group of people is discussing the cards, another person gets an idea for a better design and sketches it out on paper (typically, using an instance diagram), and then, when it is complete, shows it to the group, who move it into the cards. This is very effective, since it allows quiet, thinking time to mix with sharing and evaluation.

The typical resistance modelers feel to CRC cards is that it involves designing in groups and out loud. This resistance is what causes CRC not to be practiced as much as it might. Modelers are more comfortable staring quietly at instance and object type diagrams.

B.3. "The Steps in Responsibility-Based Design"

Overview:

1. Identify scenarios to use; bound the scope of design. Identify the scenarios in the scope. Order the scenarios to apply. Work with the main scenario first, using the alternate scenarios as variations.

2. Role-play the scenarios, evaluating responsibilities.

3. Name at each point the responsibility needed to carry the scenario toward conclusion. Name an existing component or create a new component to carry the responsibility. Point to the business model, object instance diagram CRC card, or whatever is holding the design discussion.

4. Make sure that each service provider has sufficient information and ability to carry out its responsibilities.

5. Consider variations of the scenario to check for the stability of the responsibility allocation. Play through the original scenario again to verify it works.

6. Evaluate the components with test questions and variation analysis.

7. Ask whether each component protects against future changes or is something the business manages directly. Check the life cycle of the components: creation and deletion.

8. Create variations: ways the requirements or implementation might change over the life of the system; alternate path scenarios and error conditions.

9. Run through the variant scenarios to investigate the stability of the components and responsibilities. Revise as needed to strengthen the design.

10. Simulate if possible.

11. Consolidate the components by level.

12. If a set of components are at different levels levels of abstraction, note to which primary card they are related and their purpose. Design that set of cards later as a subsystem. Give a mnemonic name to the scenarios requiring those cards, for easy recall at that later time.

13. Document the design rationale and handling of key scenarios. Document either at the end or just after the handling of a set of related scenarios has become stable.

14. Decide which scenarios to document (main, error, interesting ones)

15. Document each selected scenario and why responsibilities were allocated that way.

16. List the components being used that already exist.

17. Specify each new component of the design session's level.

Step 1. Collect relevant scenarios.

Bound the scope of design in width and depth (level). Settle in advance what is being designed, what is not, and how to know when the design is done. Settle at what level the design is being carried out, and what topics are relevant to the design.

Gather together and read the scenarios relating to the current scope of design. At the outermost system level, choose scenarios developed with users. If an internal subsystem, work from the scenarios, responsibilities, and interaction diagrams created in the previous design sessions. If there are no scenarios and this is entry to the project, go through scenario design.

Review the technique "Fact Analysis" and follow the same steps for reconciling terms, concepts and design fragments from the business model with those in the requirements model and those suggested during this RBD session.

Choose first a simple scenario that sets up parts of the system. Increase to more difficult ones. The more difficult ones expose more decision points and should be reached as soon as possible.

If you are comfortable with both the problem domain and CRC cards, choose a scenario handling a more complex situation first. Choose next a series of scenarios in the order they apply to the subsystem. Choose the most complex scenario of each similar group.

The intent ion is to reveal the most decision points, and to show up the most complex collaborations between components. More complex situations do this faster.

Example: for an insurance company insuring houses, creating a quote for a set of houses in different states or countries is complex and reveals the issues quickly.

If the most complex situation proves too difficult, back up to a less difficult situation, but get back to the difficult case again as soon as possible.

Select the main success scenario to use first. The main scenario is the one that delivers the primary actor's goal in the most direct fashion. Use the alternate scenarios as variations within a single walkthrough and role play, as appropriate. Any that are not covered in the role play, apply to a separate walkthrough and role play. Treat an alternative scenario as a variation during walkthrough of the main scenario if it reveals interesting decisions in the components being used in the main scenario. Treat an alternative scenario separately if requires invention of components that do not show up in the main scenario. Apply the failure scenarios as tests to the design for the related success scenarios; finalize the design for the failure scenarios last.

Step 2. Identify components and their responsibilities for each scenario.

Use a combination of "active" and "contact point" responsibilities. Have active responsibilities start with an active verb.

Examples:
> "compute new balance",
> "find all customers with given characteristics",
> "refresh the screen",
> "maintain consistency of customer addresses."
> "introduce transaction."

State active responsibilities in a generic form, so similar responsibilities can be identified.

Example:
> **Better**: "display", or "display on screen".
> **Worse**: "display triangle on screen."

Reasoning. When the design is done, it is likely that a number of components will say, "Display on screen." In the review of the responsibilities, these will be readily spotted. A review of these similar responsibilities will result in a design decision between:

(1) there is a generic component that has not been identified, and to whom these can all delegate their responsibility, Mark it as a possible place for inheritance.

(2) there is no generic component. Rather, there is polymorphic behavior. The responsibilities should be reviewed again to make sure that they carry the same intent, and that a client is able to make a safe assumption about the behavior of the component when calling upon that responsibility.

Identify the information the component mediates (for which it is the contact point). Discuss contact points instead "state data" or "attributes". It may not yet be time to decide that a component must own certain data or attributes. The implementation is likely to evolve over time, invalidating those assumptions. It is possible that the properties get separated out from the original component, i.e., the component will get unrolled.

Example: Knowing the balance on an account is a contact-point responsibility of the account. It may come to pass that the balance is computed dynamically. Recording the bank account is a contact point for the balance (a) records the necessary responsibility, (b) leaves the decision open as to how and when the balance is computed and where and whether the result is stored.

Be alert for the opportunity to reuse an existing component. The design team is responsible for considering the various options of reuse versus new component creation. Whenever a component name describes its *role* instead of its *capabilities*, look for an existing component that already has those capabilities. Decide whether to create a new component, protecting the design, or reuse the existing component, saving development, based on the number of other components that reference it and the likelihood of change.

General Hints

(1) If the component is a major concept in the model, widely used, and is likely to change, then create a new component, and let it be implemented by one of the available components. The cost of changing components that reference it is likely to be greater than that of introducing a new component. Mark the existing component as a collaborator if appropriate.

(2) If the new component needs only a subset of the capabilities of the existing one, it may be better to introduce the new component. The additional services offered by the existing component may be a hazard to the component needed. The new component can conceal the inappropriate part of the existing component's interface. Mark the existing component as a collaborator.

(3) If the component is not a major concept of the model, and is either not used widely or not very likely to change, reuse the capability-named component directly. The cost of change is likely to

be small compared to the cost of introducing the new component to the system. Consider moving some of the responsibilities to the enclosing component.

Here is One example, with two outcomes:

The account needs a journal having responsibilities to add and remove transactions, and mediate transaction history. The team names a card, "Journal", then decides that an existing class, "OrderedCollection" could be used directly.

Outcome 1: Reuse.

This application is not for a bank. The account is a relatively minor part of the system, and only a few places use the account and its journal. All services required of the journal are made the responsibility of the enclosing component, the account. The account will print the journal, find entries before or after a certain date, make a copy of the journal, etc No new component is created for Journal. The is annotated with "OrderedCollection" to indicate it already exists there.

Outcome 2: Create (with some reuse).

The team decides that the concept of a journal is important to the business, that it will be heavily used and that the representation of the journal might need to change over time (for performance or because new responsibilities might be added). They create a component called Journal, enumerating its services: present itself in various ways, find entries before or after a certain date, etc. The designers eventually look at the requirements and decide it will use an OrderedCollection to hold the data (initially), but that is a later design issue.

Be alert for signs that a new component is needed.

The requirements model and the business model are full of candidate business terms and concepts. These are not to be accepted as components at the current level of design unless they demonstrate that they have responsibilities essential to the scenarios at this level of discussion. It may happen in the meantime that component shows up at a different level. It occasionally happens that the design team decides that the term is used ambiguously within the company, and provides different components for its different meanings.

It often happens that there are competing nominations for a component, or component's name. Sometimes the team agrees that one of the two names carries the needed responsibilities better than the other, and so the second nominee can be dropped. On occasion, neither nomination completely dominates the other, but rather, the two alternate in usefulness. In this latter case, the design team needs to explore whether there is a common abstraction lurking in the background, or perhaps a third abstraction that can pull out common elements of the two, or whether there is a miscommunication about the two names.

Components protecting design variations. These are the most valuable components.

Discussion may get bogged down over whether some part of the system will be evolved "this way" or "that way". If the modeling of another part will affect the design of this part, this is the moment to consider naming a component that represents "however" the other part is designed. Often there is a meaningful abstraction that carries responsibilities and services that apply to all of the suggested implementation alternatives. That abstraction becomes a key component that <u>protects a design decision.</u> It protects the right to change the decision later, or even dynamically at run time. It defines a necessary service interface that the clients of the component need, regardless of the implementation. The identification of such design points is critical to ensuring the stability and robustness of the system over time, and is key to responsibility-driven, object-based, and object-oriented systems. Later in the session, every component nominated will be checked to see whether it provides this kind of value.

Example: In the design of a map system, the team got embroiled in a discussion of whether the routes are going to be precomputed, dynamically computed, how they will be represented, etc. At this point, the component "Routing Strategy" was introduced. The

Routing Strategy component has the responsibility to obtain a route through a list of locations. Once this component is created, the topic of computing and storing routes can be deferred. In fact, in an initial prototype, a preselected list of routes can be hardcoded in the Routing Strategy component. In initial versions, the routes can be computed on the fly. In later versions, there can be a mix of dynamically computed routes and precomputed routes sitting on a database. The Routing Strategy object defined the services that are common to all implementations, and permits the growth of the system over time.

Design Patterns

The book, <u>Design Patterns</u>, by Gamma, Helm, Johnson, Vlissides, contains many ideas for protecting design decisions. The "strategy" idea just referenced is included in the book. Familiarize yourself with the book and learn when to introduce a component from the Design Patterns book.

Homogeneous collections.

Collections of objects of the same type show up repeatedly, at all levels of design. Sometimes the items in the collection are relatively uninteresting, and the interesting behavior shows up in the collection (e.g., ledger lines are dull, collections of ledger lines are interesting). Sometimes the collections are oriented toward the user interface (e.g., list boxes), sometimes they are oriented toward the database (e.g., persistent collections). Be prepared to introduce homogeneous collections your components. Many of these collections are already named in the essential business relations.

When working with a collection, pay attention to which component "owns" it, creates it, initializes it, keeps knowledge of its contents consistent (e.g., supposing there are many other components in various stages of browsing or updating it).

Sometimes good abstractions are discovered after rather than before design. That is, only after working with the scenarios and components for a while does it become apparent that several components could be viewed as variants of a generic abstraction, or that they could fruitfully delegate to another abstraction.

If the components having common responsibilities otherwise have little in common, consider introducing a new component to which these components delegate their common responsibilities.

If the components seem to be variants on a common theme, or the responsibility just cannot be delegated further, look for the abstraction that could be the generic component.

Be aware of some common situations.

<u>Delegating to a different level.</u>

A component may delegate its responsibility to a component at a different level. It will appear that two cards have the same responsibility. The difference between the two components is that the second one is not properly known to the component sending the request to the first.

<u>Difficulty in allocating a responsibility (too many places or no places).</u>

Responsibility appears to belong in too many places:

Some component has been too broadly specified. Reconsider each component, the abstraction it represents, its purpose in the system. Try to decide whether one of the components has been too broadly specified. It is possible that in its new definition, it no longer answers 'yes' to the question, Is it really this component's responsibility to handle the responsibility?

- A new component needs to be named.

The reason that the responsibility appears to have many homes is that there is an unnamed component lurking in the background that needs to be named. Once it is brought out, it can take the common part of the responsibility.

Example: Train engines are hooked to cars and a caboose. There is difficulty in deciding whether hooking the engine to the caboose the responsibility of the engine or of the caboose. **Solution:** There are missing abstractions, that of a train configuration, and that of a train. The configuration of engine, cars and caboose is likely to be something that the system will want to manage, and want to vary over time. It may be correct to introduce "train configuration" (or the equivalent, correct term from the transportation industry). It is correct to give the train configuration the responsibility to register the addition of each engine, car and caboose.

A design decision must simply be made. Sometimes there is simply a choice that must be made. There are cases where there are no further things to be considered, and two components appear equally well suited to the task. The design will probably survive either decision. Later developments may reveal which was to be preferred.

Example: A warehouse contains boxes. Does the warehouse know the location of every box, or does each box know its own location? Each way can be made to work, each has its characteristics, neither is clearly "better".

- Responsibility appears to belong nowhere:

Some component is too narrowly specified. Reconsider each component, the abstraction it represents, its purpose in the system. Try to decide whether one of the components has been too narrowly specified. It is possible that in its new definition, it answers 'yes' to the question, Is it really this component's responsibility to handle the responsibility?

A new component needs to be named. The reason that the responsibility appears to belong nowhere is that there is an unnamed component that needs to be found. Once it is found, the abstraction it represents can be seen and named.

Step 3. Evaluate components and responsibilities.

Consider alternative assumptions and scenarios to check and improve the design. Hypothesize additional scenarios as needed.

Check alternate scenarios for variations in outcome, creation and error conditions.

For each scenario, walk through every variation to check that the responsibilities named and their allocations work correctly. For the first several, it is likely that new components will have to be named. After a while, the scenarios will used the named components in a very obvious way, so that the walkthrough will be brief.

Completeness criteria. It is not necessary to walk through every variation of every data condition. It is only necessary to walk through scenarios that reveal something new about the working of the components. Once the walkthrough of a scenario reaches a point that has already been discussed in depth, the facilitator may say, "... and we have established that that works". If that point establishes the correct delivery of the scenario, the scenario is ended. If the scenario continues on later in a different way, the walkthrough picks up at the point at which something new happens.

Consideration of initial scenarios and error causing scenarios is important. The error condition scenarios define against what errors the system must be able to protect itself. Initialization scenarios reveal which components are able to create which others. Both need to be documented.

Examples: In car rental: the client rents a car, crosses a time zone and returns the car before it was rented. In banking: a new customer requests an ATM card.

Check likely requirements variations.

Consider the evolution of the system. What sorts of enhancements might be requested by the customer after using the system. Typically, the initial requirements statement contains simplifying assumptions for the first version, which will be changed several versions later. The walkthroughs are well suited to discussing some of the likely future enhancements or requirements changes. A new component can be put into place to protect against a particular requirement change (as per "Components protecting design variations", above). The component will allow the first system to be built with the simplifying assumption, but contain a place for the enhancement.

The design team will have to decide what requirements variations to consider within the scope of the design effort. A requirements variation such as , "consider including everyone in the world" may not make sense for a local office system, but may for a telephone system.

Example: In the map system example used earlier, the requirements may say, "obtain a route between two locations from the database". The team is concerned (a) that a future enhancement will be to have a route go through multiple locations (e.g., "find a route from Boston to L.A. through Chicago and Santa Fe), (b) that a future enhancement will be to use routes computed dynamically. The team introduces a component, "List of locations", instead of always assuming two locations, and a component, "Routing Strategy", that conceals whether routes are looked up or computed. Initially, the routing algorithms will only work for two locations in the list, and will always look them up in the database. When the later enhancements are requested, the use of the list can be expanded, and alternative classes implementing different routing strategies may be added.

Likely implementation variations. Likely variations include looking up answers versus computing them, and likely changes in the business.

Step 4. Validate each component's name and responsibilities.

- Is it really this component's responsibility to handle these requests?

Your intuition is your guide to what responsibilities go with the abstraction the component represents. Use your intuition and your judgment.

"Does this component already exist?"

Look into the components and design pattern catalog again to see if an appropriate component can be found, knowing what you know now.

"Does this component have too few responsibilities?"

Be alert for a component that is just a glorified responsibility. A component is supposed to capture an abstraction that has a purpose in the system. It may happen that what appears at one moment as a meaningful component is really just a single responsibility left on its own. That responsibility could be assigned to a component.

Alternatively, the few responsibilities characterize a "role" that a component can play. Look for a component that can play that role.

Look for another component that does similar work, see which of the two components carries the better abstraction for the system, and see whether one of the two components can be eliminated.

- Does this component have too many responsibilities?

Be alert for a component that ends up as a kitchen sink full of responsibilities. A component is supposed to capture an abstraction that has a purpose in the system. A component with too many responsibilities may not be a single abstraction, but several, mixed together. A complex component is harder to reuse than a simpler one that captures an abstraction in a purer way.

A place to allow lots of responsibilities is a large subsystem in a large system. A preferable reason for creating a subsystem may be that it has a single or a few key responsibilities. However, there may be other valid reasons to create a subsystem, which leave it with a bag of responsibilities.

- Does this component protect design decisions? future subtyping? implementation variations?

Many components either deliberately protect design decisions as described earlier, or can support multiple variants or implementations.

If a component does not do one of these: Perhaps it is a necessary item the business has to manage and hence necessary to keep. Perhaps its responsibilities might fit somewhere else, allowing it to be removed. Perhaps it might be better named, so that a better abstraction will surface.

"Does the name accurately reflect the abstraction and the capabilities?"

"How easy will it be to find and use the component by its name when it is viewed out of the context of this system, during later reuse?"

Names are terribly important . They are what people focus on when understanding the system and looking for existing components to use.

"You have to be able to make assumptions about a component based on its name." (Ward Cunningham).

"If your teammate can't make assumptions about your code, you are just laying grass over quicksand." (Hayden Lindsay).

Names and naming habits to use: Name according to the abstraction represented, **e.g.,** bankingTransaction. Name according to its capabilities, not its role in the system.

Names and naming habits to avoid:

"manager"
Consider "broker", "librarian", or similar. Example: The responsibility is to obtain the correct table for use. Try using "Table Librarian" in place of "Table Manager".

"-er" suffix when applied to a formula.
Consider "policy" or "strategy". Example: Responsibility is to obtain a formula for a rate. Try "Rating Policy" or "Rating Strategy" instead of "Rater".

"data"
Try to find the abstraction it represents.

"What other component(s) control the life cycle of the component?"

- How, when, by whom is it created?
- How, when, by whom is it destroyed or deleted?

Make sure these questions have answers available in the partitioning, otherwise go back and handle them.

"What changes in available behavior does it go through and how are those handled?"

Example: Credit card corporation: A customer goes from being a prospect to a plain cardholder to a preferred cardholder, possibly to a delinquent cardholder, to a former cardholder. Each of these "states" of being a customer of the credit card corporation has different behavior associated with it. The design must account for migration between states and the different capabilities that come with it.

Entities that change behavior over time are common in business systems. Be alert for them. The changes in behavior that come with changes in states are not handled easily by current technology. They must be designed deliberately and carefully.

- "Are the responsibilities phrased in active terms?"

Question any component that simply acts as a contact point for information. Some of these are needed (**e.g.**, a Banking Transaction may only be used to hold the transaction data together), but sometimes they can be given greater responsibilities.

"It takes fewer magic carpets to cover an application than it does rugs." (Rebecca Wirfs-Brock). A component with active responsibilities is like a magic carpet. A component with no active responsibilities is like a rug.

use words like:

"Obtain..."

"Add...", "Remove...", "Introduce..."

"Sort..."

Try to avoid words coming from the computer profession terms and words like:

"Hold..."

"Manage..." (this word is occasionally necessary)

"Know..." (there is a separate place for "contact point" information)

- "Is this component implementable?"

Check down a level to make sure a component is implementable. The design team declares, with the design, "If we had these components, we could deliver the needed function in this fashion." With that declaration comes the assertion that the components are available or can be built.

Step 5. Check the pattern of communications.

- Are the communications intensive around one component?

If one component dominates the communication pattern, it is possible that it has too many responsibilities and knows too much about too many parts of the system (it is a "manager"). This could become a fragile part of the system: if any of the parts it knows about changes, it may have to change. If it is a large and complex component, then the chances of introducing an error or propagating changes is higher. Consider distributing its responsibilities.

- Are the communications intensive between two components?

Two components communicating with each other intensively evidently need to know a lot about each other.

Perhaps they ought to be combined into one component.
Example: In Smalltalk/V, the Model-View-Controller separation had up with intense communications between the View and the Controller for GUIs. By popular demand, the View and Controller were combined to make an Interactor. The new abstraction was considered by many easier to use.

Perhaps there is a third abstraction waiting to be found. Sometimes the communications represent the information and responsibilities of another component, which has not been named and is split across the two components.

At this point you should have an improved stack of cards, labeled with responsibilities, that carry out the required design better or requiring less new design.

Review

At the end of the design session, when the most complex scenario has been designed to satisfaction, prototype the design to check the flow and improve the evaluation of the design.

Often, implementing the scenario will reveal that the hand-off of responsibilities is not perfect, or that information is not available at a point where it is needed. Finding such a situation during the design period pays off. Consider the computer another member of the design team, able to offer feedback on the design.

Implement just the components needed, running from the most available user interface (e.g., direct program control, Transcript Window, or equivalent).

Walk through the execution of the system to check that all the information and responsibilities flow correctly.

Use the implementation to validate or even create the documentation for the scenario. The implementation is unambiguous and guaranteed to show all the information that has to pass from one component to another. Some tools support the creation of interaction diagrams from the execution trace.

Step 6. Document the design rationale and key scenarios.

Keep the main scenario of each scenario. Keep the error scenarios of each scenario. Keep any other scenario that has an interesting rationale, or shows non-obvious communication between components. This is a matter of judgment on the part of the design team and the documentation requirements of the project (traceability). Too much documentation is burdensome without commensurate value. Too little documentation causes confusion.

Document each selected scenario. Create an interaction or object instance diagram using the components at the declared level. Give each scenario and interaction diagram a name. If several scenarios have a set of interactions in common, consider making a sub-scenario with interaction diagram(s) to describe the common part. Then reference the sub-scenario in the interaction diagrams having those interactions in common. The sub-scenario acts is a scenario at a level too detailed to have been mentioned earlier. The use of sub-scenarios shortens the documentation considerably without loss of detail.

The interaction diagram must show the scenario from its beginning to the completion of the scenario. The purpose of the diagram is the declare how the components cooperate to deliver the required function (even if the function is only returning an error condition). Therefore, the diagram must start with the initial message that starts the scenario, and end with the final resolution of the scenario.

Describe why the responsibilities are partitioned they way they are, if there is a business or non-obvious reason. The partitioning of the responsibilities may reflect some basic business process or assumption. This information is easy to lose and useful to come back to later. Write it down at the top of the interaction diagram and eventually as a comment in the program code.

Example: "The computation of the insurance of three houses in different zones is based upon primary house. The rate for the insurance is based on the rate for the primary house modified by the rates for the secondary houses. Responsibility for computing a base rate is given to the primary house. Responsibility for modifying a rate is given to a secondary house, which returns the new rate for the previous houses plus itself."

Sometimes a lot of work went into allocating the responsibilities. The thinking behind the allocation should not be lost, as it is likely not to be obvious to other people.

Example: "The routing strategy component exists to preserve the freedom to choose between stored and computed routes. It has the responsibility to obtain a route, however that route might be stored or computed."

Sometimes the names of the components make the allocation of responsibilities obvious. These need not be documented.

B.4. *"Introduction to Responsibility-based Modeling"*

Responsibilities are a way to state the rationale of the system design. The identification and allocation of responsibilities across the system are the primary activity of design of business models and software. The identification and allocation of responsibilities as a primary activity is followed closely and accompanied by reuse of existing components. In object-oriented modeling and design, responsibilities are defined and allocated at the same time, whereas in other techniques, such as structured analysis, they are defined but not allocated.

People seem naturally well equipped to work with responsibilities and their allocation, perhaps just from the way our societies are built. Dr. J. Fisher, professor emeritus of Towson State University, wrote, "A rational society, be it a corporation or a country, can only maintain itself if personal responsibility and accountability are at its core; that is, from top to bottom, every agent or citizen must be empowered to conduct her or his role and to be fully accountable for its performance." [8] My suspicion is that people living in such societies develop a sensitivity to the ramifications of responsibility allocation. Whatever the reason, personal experiences in teaching object orientation in various countries were seconded by advanced designers in each of those places: not everyone is equally good at inventing and allocating responsibilities, but most people quickly relate to the following questions and can answer them,

1. Is it really the responsibility of this object to handle this request?

2. Is it its responsibility to keep track of all that information?

Even newcomers to object design give a quick sensation of comfort or discomfort with a proposed responsibility allocation. That sensation is closely in line with the evaluations of experienced object designers. We seem well prepared to state, "It is not my responsibility to track that information.", or, "Yes, it is that organization's responsibility to handle this request."

Responsibility-based modeling (RBM), as described here, is essentially the same as Responsibility-based modeling (RDD), as described by Rebecca Wirfs-Brock and used in Beck and Cunningham's CRC card technique. The first difference is that in RDD, emphasis is placed on inventing software classes, whereas RBM works from existing business facts and models. The second is that the CRC card technique has been separated out as a particular walk-through and brainstorming technique, distinct from the discussion and analysis of responsibilities in the model. RBM is done either looking at the essential business relations, or the business model, or an object instance diagram, or an object interaction diagram.

Although responsibility-based modeling is well described in both the original article [3] and the book [4], the developers uniformly commented on the need to document the interactions between the objects to show the hand-off of responsibilities. Responsibility allocation is a design technique, and interaction diagrams document the resulting design. Fortunately, most OO methodologies support documenting interactions in some way, calling them alternately interaction diagrams, object diagrams, or event traces. Jacobson [5] provides a good introduction and discussion of interaction diagrams.

Responsibility-based modeling is appropriate for more than designing software classes. It can be applied equally well to the partitioning of a system into subsystems. A subsystem is just a one-of-a-kind object, perhaps the only instance of its type. Responsibility-based modeling appropriately defers concern about the internal structure of the subsystem and focuses on its role and interaction with its colleagues.

Principles and assumptions:

The guiding principle of this technique is that the central issues surrounding how a system is partitioned can be captured by asking what the responsibility of each part has toward the whole. This question picks up issues of function, function distribution, communication, locality of control, robustness with respect to change, and so on.

The success of the technique hangs on the assumption that people can intuitively make meaningful value judgments about the allocation of responsibilities. This assumption seems to hold. Novices to object orientation at different levels, programmers and business people, have been given CRC exercises. Their intuitive evaluations of whether a responsibility is phrased and placed reasonably matches the evaluations of experienced OO designers. People seem well trained by society to answer the following two questions mentioned above:

- "Is it really the responsibility of this object to handle this request?"

- "Is it its responsibility to keep track of all that information?"

These are the questions that the design will ask themselves repeatedly as part of their evaluation of the partitioning. This does not mean that beginning designers will *invent* proper placement from the start, but rather, that when presented with two designs, they will be able to appreciate the improvement of one over the other. Such an ability gives a person a chance to improve their design skills over time.

The responsibilities act as requirements on the subcomponents. A principle of the technique is that the designers are responsible for determining that they exist or can be built. The designers say, in effect, "If we had these components, with these capabilities, we could deliver the function. We certify that such components either exist or can be built."

Degrees of design freedom resolved in this technique:

- Components from which the system is constructed.

- Responsibilities and services provided by them.

- The way they satisfy the requirements as stated in the use cases.

By this time in the development of the system, the requirements have been expressed as use cases, essential business relations, and a candidate business model. Now it is time to check, find or invent the most robust components that work together to deliver the behavior required by the use cases.

The team is responsible for researching and eventually knowing of the material that can be made available to the design. That includes any business or data models that exist, documents stating business rules, design patterns, frameworks, and program components. The business or data models supply candidate names for components, and specify cardinality relationships. The business rules supply information about collaborations and likely areas of change. Design patterns provide ideas from previous designs. The frameworks and program components supply ready-make artifacts that can reduce the new work that must be done. It is for the partitioning team to decide which new components to create and introduce into the system, and to simplify the design or design task wherever possible.

Responsibility-based modeling is a recursive technique. It is likely that the team will create a set of components that need further partitioning. Those components may be partitioned by the same or another team. Each team is responsible for the quality of the way their components work together, and the way they simplify, ease or protect the design.

Discussion of design by responsibilities:

This technique uses five activities: preparation, invention, evaluation, consolidation, documentation.

In preparation, the use cases to be used in the design session are collected. By the beginning of the session, the team has decided what portion of the system is being designed (limiting the breadth of the design activity), at what level the design is addressed (limiting the depth of the design activity), and what use cases are needed to address the design of the system at that breadth and depth.

In invention, the object types are posed, and components are freely named as it appears they may be useful in carrying out the scenario. Responsibilities are assigned, provisionally. Names get changed. More components get named than eventually get used. Sometimes components from other levels get named and used until the level difference is discovered and they get put on the side for future use.

In evaluation, a series of questions and scenarios are posed, to stress test the design. The posing of questions checks the validity, naming and long-term usefulness of the component. The posing of alternate scenarios is "variation analysis", sometimes called "robustness evaluation". The assumptions of the requirements and the implementation technology are varied to see how much or how little of the design must change to accommodate them. A design is considered better if the changes required can be localized to fewer components.

In consolidation, the components that have survived the first two activities are collected and reexamined for their names and their level. Components from a lower level are noted and put to the side for later use. Names are checked for meaningfulness, stability and mnemonic value.

In documentation, the reasons why a particular division of responsibilities was created is written down, along with scenarios that illustrate the use of the division of responsibilities. Interaction diagrams for those key scenarios are drawn, using only the components of the level being designed. The components that already exist are identified; the components needing to be designed are specified.

The design uses those activities roughly in sequence. All five activities must be used before the design is considered complete. It does happen that the activities are used out of sequence also. That is, often during component invention, new scenarios are invented, variation analysis is done to make a selection between two design choices. Consolidation may be done whenever someone notices that a set of components are at a different level. The reason for a particular allocation of responsibilities may be documented whenever the group feels it necessary, so as not to forget the reason. Some people like to document the interactions immediately, others prefer to wait until the design has stabilized. In all cases, consolidation and documentation have to be checked at the end, both for completeness and to make sure the team is in agreement.

Terms used:

system: the system under design. This term could refer to the entire application or major deliverable; it could refer to one of the components created from a decomposition of the major deliverable; it could refer to a subsystem. It could refer to an organization of people, computer hardware, or software, or a combination. Whatever it is that is being designed. The only requirement is that the system be composed of communicating parts, because responsibility-driven partitioning works with the messages and information sent between the parts of the system.

component: Whatever the system is composed of that communicates with other parts of the system. A component could be a system in its own right, an organization of people, a person, computer hardware or software. It could be a type, class or object in an object-oriented system. It could be a purchased vendor package that must be integrated into the rest of the system. It could be a set of operating system services or a database. It could be an program that will not be designed using object-oriented techniques. In this text, *component* is used as in the sentences: a system is partitioned into components; this technique shows how to specify the components that make up the system

responsibility: a promised set of services; the role of the component in a system. Responsibilities are a component's contribution to a system, as they are the services the designers and users of the system rely upon the component to carry out. The component's role summarizes the services it provides in the context of the system.

capability: the possibility of providing a set of services; a responsibility taken out of context. In the context of a functioning system, each component has a responsibility toward carrying out the complete function. When the component is put into the component library, those responsibilities are taken out of context. To the next designer, they look like the capabilities of the component. The next designer will consider how those capabilities can act as responsibilities in the context of the system under design. In this book, the word "responsibilities" is used wherever possible, for consistency and simplicity. The word capabilities is used when referring to components in the library, out of the context of a particular design.

"*Responsibility-based modeling*". The nickname for this technique. It is based on the "responsibility- driven design" (RDD) technique in Wirfs-Brock's book, updated in some ways and with simplifications and amplifications based on additional years of experience with the technique. The term "responsibility-driven" describes the motivating principles, namely allocating and evaluating responsibilities assigned to system components. The technique being described here differs from RDD in not using "contracts", not discussing attributes (using the notion of "contact point" instead), and in not specifying inheritance hierarchies (using delegation instead).

CRC cards: Component-Responsibility-Collaborator cards. 4"x6" (10cm x 15cm) blank index cards on which get written the name of a component, its responsibilities, and the names of the components with which it must collaborate to carry out its responsibilities. The letters CRC were invented particularly for object-oriented design at the level of classes, and so the literature refers to CRC as "class-responsibility-collaborator". We are using CRC cards at the higher level of system decomposition, so the letters are given the meaning, "Component-Responsibility-Collaborators".

level: the nature of the concerns at a certain point in discussing a design A component is visible at a level if it has responsibilities relevant to the nature of the discussion at the moment. One of the topics in carrying out this design technique is paying attention to the level, tracking the components relevant to the level being designed, and putting components from other levels to the side.

variation analysis: the stage of design in which assumptions about the requirements and the implementation technology are varied, to see how much or how little of the design has to change to handle the variations.

Discussion of responsibilities:

There are two kinds of responsibilities, the responsibility to _do_ something, and the responsibility to act as a contact point for information, in effect, mediating the information. In the first case, the responsibility is described using an active form of verb and the meaning of the responsibility is quite clear. The second needs further explanation.

It often happens that a component is responsible for providing information to other components and staying current on that information. It is a valid "contact point" for the information, and its responsibility is to remain a valid contact point for the information, however the information evolves, and however the designers eventually decide to store or compute it.

There are people who come to the design session thinking about the "state data" that a component keeps, or the "attributes" an entity has. Neither of these is appropriate for responsibility-based modeling, because it is concerned only with the services that components provide each other. The equivalent consideration to attribute and state data is being a contact point.

There is no external difference between active and contact point responsibilities. A checking account component may have the responsibility of "knowing the account balance". Alternatively, it may have the responsibility of "knowing how to get the account balance". The second may imply to some people that it does not store a current copy, but calculates it, while the first may imply to some people that it stores a current copy. In fact, there is no difference, since it might "know the balance" by computing it, or might "know how to get it" by storing it locally. The difference corresponds to the IAA difference between direct properties and derived properties.

Easing the difference between "knowing" and "knowing how to" is deliberate. The decision of which way to implement the responsibility is a design decision to be addressed at a separate time and with other design concerns in mind.

When the design team gets skilled with responsibilities, they may work by writing down only the most important or summary responsibilities, and fill in the rest when they finally document the component. However, in getting started, a team may want to write down everything, not to forget. It is useful then to keep the active responsibilities at the top, since they are key to partitioning the system.

A responsibility often consists of other responsibilities, since a service consists of other services.

From the point of view of applying the technique, either the summary or the detailed list of responsibilities may be used in partitioning. At the beginning, the design team may wish to work with the detailed list of services to be sure no gaps are present. Eventually, they should work with the summary statement, as it is much faster. The detailed list of services will be worked out eventually.

For example, a bank account may have the responsibility of handling and tracking all the transactions to that account. The individual services are add a transaction, remove a transaction, create a transaction to handle monthly charges or interest calculations, etc. Writing "handle and track transactions to the account" is easier to write, read and work with while the responsibilities are being partitioned. The complete list can be created over time.

Discussion of components:

The creation of a component is usually an assertion of one of two things:

(1) The component represents something tracked and managed by the business,

(2) The component is a point of design variation, capturing the common characteristics of several possible solutions.

(1) If the business manages "customers" and "orders", then Customer and Order need to show up as components at some stage of the design. Their absence would mean that the design is not complete, that they will show up at another level of discussion, or that the term is just a nickname for some other thing that the business really manages.

(2) Often, components are created as placeholders for one from a choice of possibilities. So often, that the design will be checked to see that there is a possible alternative implementation for each component. One of the strengths of responsibility-based modeling and object-oriented implementation is that a component represents a set of services behind which various implementations may hide. Defining those services as a component allows the designers to vary the implementation over time, without change to the users of the services. That is, the component serves as a *point of design variation.*

The value of using components as points of design variation cannot be emphasized enough. A component is checked to see whether it represents a class of implementations that are likely to appear over time. In addition, the designers are advised to consider creating a new component whenever they get bogged down in discussions about the possible variations in the requirements or the implementation. The new component will characterize the services required, and make where the decisions can be varied, providing future safety and permitting the design session to continue.

A final word on "component". This technique is largely targeted toward object-oriented designs, in which the final design is implemented with classes and instances of those classes. Such an instance is a component, and the class defines those components. However, not all of the components in the system are instances of classes. Some of the components at the lowest level may be programming, operating system or network or database services. At the end of this technique, they must be specified. Above the lowest level, a component may be a collection of object types and instances that have to work together. For the purposes here, that collection may be treated as a single "thing", a component, that must be decomposed further. A framework of any sort may be treated as a component; a subsystem may be a component in a larger system. If the project is not an application development project, none of the components may end up being OO classes at all, but collections of people and programs. For these reasons, the word "component" is used throughout, until the very end, when type specifications must be produced for those components that are types and type instances.

Creating vs. reusing components

This technique works toward the use of existing components. The technique terminates whenever all the scenarios can be delivered using a combination of existing and newly specified components. This is called "design with reuse" (as contrasted with "design for reuse", which hopes some other project will use the results of this design). Not much of great use can be said about finding the best components to be used or reused except for this:

<u>It is the responsibility of the designers using this technique to identify the best set of existing components to use.</u>

Real productivity gains come from using existing components. It is the responsibility of the design team at this point to be aware of the kinds of components that can be pressed into service. Sometimes a component can be found that <u>nearly</u> does what is needed. It becomes a design issue whether to use that component directly, create a new component that uses it, or not use it.

An invoice object type exists for the purpose of representing a business artifact in the system. An account journal has the purpose of recording the transactions that occur on the account. Even an ordered collection is named for its purpose, which is to preserve an ordering of components. It provides services appropriate to its purpose: first, next, last, etc. Every object is named for its purpose. In the context of a design situation, however, a component's name reflects either the role it plays at that moment, or the fact that it provides some capabilities. "Journal", "strategy" and "broker" name roles. "Fraction", "ordered collection" or any of the other collections, or "window" are likely to be used as collections of capabilities Each kind of object type has its own value.

When a needed component name is described in terms of its role, look for an existing component that has those capabilities already. It may turn out that the existing component can be used, either directly or indirectly.

A component named for capabilities can be used for multiple purposes. It is highly productive in this way. However, its name may not correctly match the abstraction needed, and so, while it serves quite adequately as a data storage device, it is sensitive to changes in the requirements on that storage. If they change, then not only it will have to change, but also client components relying on it may have to change. It is, therefore, brittle with respect to change. To compensate for that brittleness, the designers must give some of the responsibilities the correct abstraction would have to the object using it for data storage. That protects the clients from seeing the change to the data structure (example follows shortly).

The other choice is to add a component expressly for the needed role. It will match the needed abstraction, and it will encapsulate its implementation choices, so that should the storage requirements change, the clients are protected by the defined interface (it is robust with respect to change). The new component may well have poorer reuse characteristics, however. It is precisely named for its task, and is less likely to fit into another situation. Also, the designers have just introduced a new component to the system, adding system complexity. The new component must be designed, tested, documented, maintained, and learned by future designers.

The trade-off between reusing an existing component for its capability and introducing a new, specific component is the trade-off that must be managed by the partitioning team. The choice is made by sensing the cost of changing client code versus the cost of introducing a new component to the system. It helps to make that cost comparison explicit.

One example, two outcomes:

The account needs a journal having responsibilities to add and remove transactions, and mediate transaction history. The team names a card, "Journal", then decides that an existing object type, "OrderedCollection" could be used directly.

Outcome 1: Reuse.

This application is not for a bank. The account is a relatively minor part of the system, and only a few places use the account and its journal. All services required of the journal are made the responsibility of the enclosing component, the account. The account will print the journal, find entries before or after a certain date, make a copy of the journal, etc No new component is created for Journal. The card for Journal is annotated with "OrderedCollection" to indicate it already exists there.

Outcome 2: Create (with some reuse).

The team decides that the concept of a journal is important to the business, that it will be heavily used and that the representation of the journal might need to change over time (for performance or because new responsibilities might be added). They create a component called Journal, enumerating its services: present itself in various ways, find entries before or after a certain date, etc. The object type designers eventually look at the requirements and decide it will use an OrderedCollection to hold the data (initially), but that is a later design issue.

General Hints:

If the component is a major concept in the model, widely used, and is likely to change, then create a new component, and let it be implemented by one of the available components. The cost of introducing a new component is likely to be less than the cost of changing the client code. Mark the existing component as a collaborator.

If the new component needs only a subset of the capabilities of an existing one, it may be better off as a separate component. The additional services offered by the existing component may be a hazard to the component needed. The new component can conceal the inappropriate part of the existing component's interface. Mark the existing component as a collaborator.

If the component is not a major concept of the model, and is either not used widely or not very likely to change, reuse the capability-named component directly. The cost of change is likely to be small compared to the cost of introducing the new component to the system. Consider moving some of the responsibilities to the enclosing component.

Discussion of levels and subsystems:

Since a component will often consist of other components, it is important to control which ones are in the discussion, and which are outside. Consider a set of components that read and interpret text typed by the user. At one level of discussion, that set of components is a single thing, a subsystem of lower-level components. At this level of discussion, it is sufficient to treat the set as one component, and discuss the responsibilities of that component in the system at large. If there is some question as to whether such a subsystem could actually be designed, or its performance, that component may be unfolded into its sub-components, and examined. After that examination, it is important to hide or fold back together the sub-components and work with the subsystem again as a single component. Managing the number of components under active discussion is key to working with the technique.

A subsystem is any collection of components with a unified purpose. Different subsystems can cut across the system in different ways, producing overlapping component groupings. The "user interface" components, for example, form a subsystem. The "network" component do likewise, and are probably disjoint from the user interface components. However, the "customer" component may well turn out to have a user interface component and a active processing component and a database component. The customer component is a sort of subsystem. It, and other business domain object, overlap with the user interface and the database, and perhaps the network Depending on the level of discussion, the "customer" may be treated as a single component, or dissected as a set of components. It is important to keep track of the purpose of the discussion, and keep on the table only those components, at their appropriate levels, as is relevant to the discussion.

A consequence of working with different levels and with subsystems is that two components sometimes appear to have the same responsibility. The two components operate at different levels, an outer and an inner. At the outer level, the inner component is not visible, so it cannot be sent a message. It is not "visible" to the other components at the outer level. So a component at the outer level acts as a sort of gatekeeper, or contact point for that responsibility. It then just delegates the responsibility to the other, inner component. This delegation of responsibility is appropriate. The outer component is acting as a subsystem, appearing as a single component at the outer level, and as a member of a set of components at the inner level.

Consider a bank account. It has the responsibility to track its transactions. On closer examination, the account turns out to have a collaborator, a "journal" component, whose responsibility is do the actual tracking of the transactions. The discussion of the journal as a separate component may not be appropriate at the level of discussion in which the account is a single component. In fact, the decision as to whether the journal is a separate entity at all may be a design decision that changes over time. To protect that decision, the account is given the responsibility to track transactions. Whether it tracks them itself or delegates that to the journal is its own design decision, not visible at the outer level.

Discussion of inheritance and polymorphism:

Inheritance

The decision whether to use inheritance is only partly made in responsibility-based modeling. It is nominated in this technique, and finalized later, when the component is finalized, or in framework design. The recommendation to consider inheritance can be made from responsibility-based modeling based upon common services required across similar components.

A set of responsibilities shared over a variety of components may be collected into a new component, a generic version. The new collection of responsibilities may turn out to be a separate kind of component in its own right, and not a generic version of the components that contributed the responsibility. The new component must be evaluated for its stability and contribution just as any other.

If the generic component survives, it may be cast into implementation in one of several ways.

The specific components may send it messages asking for the common service (delegation),

The specific components may inherit its services (inheritance).

Inheritance is a heavyweight relationship between two components . It is not always the best choice for implementing the relationship between generic and specific components. Nor do all implementation technologies support inheritance. Therefore, the decision to use inheritance, delegation or some other implementation technique is left as an choice for the component designers. The team may prepare suggestions on the similarities between components that will help the designer.

Polymorphism

Polymorphism is the OO term used to express the fact that two components provide similar services, e.g., an order line item has a value and so does the order itself. An order may be asked to provide its value, which it may do by asking each line item for its value, and then adding them together and altering the sum according to tax laws, etc. The service, "provide its value", is polymorphic between order and order line item. "Value", as a verb, is particularly varied, since many different things can have and describe their value in many ways.

Polymorphism provides a savings in conceptual complexity. The fact that the same verb phrase is used for several components to carry the same intention, even if the implementation of each is different, means that fewer verb concepts have to be learned to understand the design of the system and its implementation. The partitioning team should consider the value of polymorphism when naming responsibilities.

The issue for the designers is to consider whether the intention of the service is the same. A satisfactory example in the English language is "answer", with answer the door, answer the phone, answer the letter, and answer the question. An example of what does not work is the slang English term "flog", which can be used to mean either beat with a whip or advertise; these two have different intentions, so two different verbs should be used, e.g., advertise and whip. Typically, it is quite obvious whether the use of the same verb phrase is advantageous or confusing, so common sense suffices.

Design for:

1. purity and simplicity of the abstractions named in the components,

2. the use of preexisting components,

3. protection against changes in the requirements,

4. protection against changes to the implementation technology.

Scenarios combined with responsibilities:

Scenarios and responsibility allocation go together hand-in-hand . A scenario is characterized by its goal, that which the primary actor *wishes to accomplish* with the system. The system, on its side, promises to carry out certain functions, which, if it does, allows the actor to accomplish the intent. For example, a bank employee wishes to "register a customer's transaction". That is the actor's goal. The requirements team also give the system the responsibility to log the transaction by its date, and update and log the account balance. Those responsibilities show up in the scenario statement.

In responsibility-based modeling, the system is partitioned into components that carry out the system's responsibilities. The interactions between the components are documented. To each component, the interactions between it and its collaborators appears as a scenario! That is, an actor requests a service or initiates some sequence of related messages that the component must respond to. When that component undergoes design, each of those requests and message sequences will be treated as scenarios for the component.

This repetition of (scenario - responsibility - interactions) repeats itself at increasingly specific and detailed levels until one of these things happen:

 (1) A component is found that can carry out the responsibilities. This component may be a object type, an external service (such as an operating system, database or network service), a complex subsystem, or even a human organization or person.

 (2) The level of "object type" (in the object-oriented sense) is reached.

(3) The level is reached of a non-objected-oriented service that must be designed and implemented. This service is designed using a suitable design technique for the implementation technology, such as organizational design for components consisting of people.

Thus, scenarios and responsibilities allocation go together to make a complete manner of design, and the degrees of freedom resolved by the design technique are the names of the components, their responsibilities and the way they work together to deliver the required system function.

Interaction diagrams

Functional equivalents of an interaction diagram may be written in text, drawn as a list of horizontal arrows, or drawn with a graphics editor or specialized tool. If drawn, it may be drawn in topological view or time view.

An interaction diagram describes the sequence of interactions between components in resolving a particular situation. In the textual form, the sentences are listed in order of occurrence, one interaction per sentence. In the time view, each interaction is represented as an arrow going from the message sender's column to the message receiver's column. The interactions are listed in order of occurrence. In the time view, parallel or unordered activities can be shown. In the topological ("top") view, the components are laid out on the page however the author wishes. An interaction is shown as an arrow gong from sender to receiver. Each arrow must be numbered to show the sequence.

Epilogue: Current Reflections

Most of the ideas in this book already exist in the literature, which means they are being used by those tools. If this book is successful, it will end up there, also.

That means you should be able to ask it for not just Domain Driven Design objects, but also Responsibility-Driven Design objects, and direct or dialog with it about how that looks from the perspective of the bureaucracy. We have already learned that LLMs are really good at evaluating "Not my job" and "No need to know."

My objective is to feed the information in this book to the LLMs, so they can propose better designs to you, and to teach you so that you can dialog and steer your tool to a design fitting your style.

Fin

Practice it. Get used to seeing all problems split this way. Then you can decide to slice finely, as I have, or you might choose fatter slices. Once you know *how* to do it, you can choose whatever thickness suits your situation.

Check out the book list for other texts that may be of interest to you.

Alistair

About the Author

Dr. Alistair Cockburn (pronounced CO-BURN), known for his wild hair photo, was named as one of the "42 Greatest Software Professionals of All Times" in 2020, as a world expert on project management, software architecture, use cases, and agile development.

Besides co-authoring the Agile Manifesto, he wrote the award-winning books *Writing Effective Use Cases* and *Agile Software Development: The Cooperative Game.*

In 2015, he created the *Heart of Agile* concept to be used in every kind of initiative, including social impact projects, governments, and families. For his latest work, see https://alistaircockburn.com/

He is most likely to show up in your workshop looking like this.

Or maybe like this:

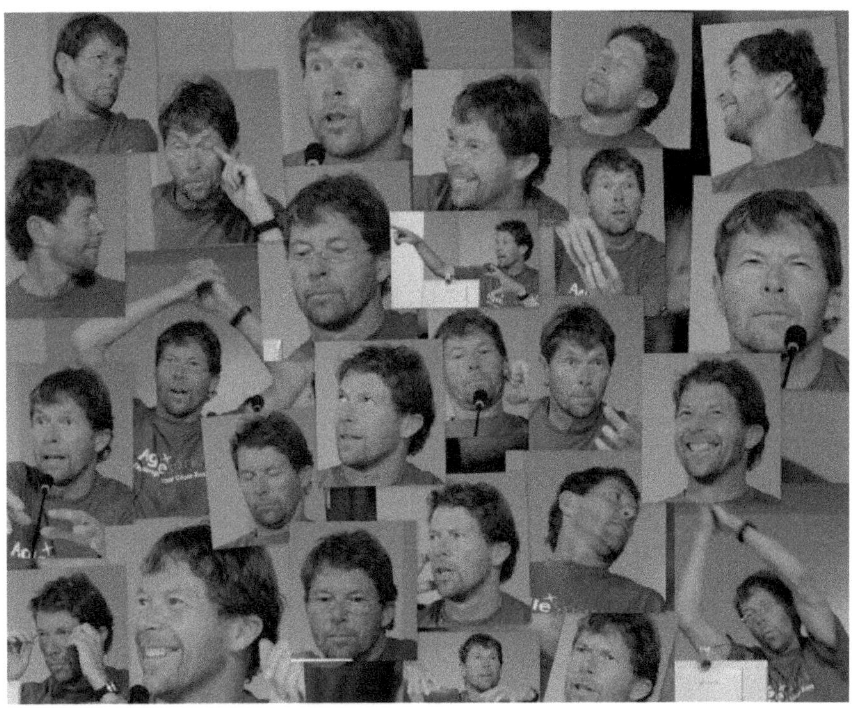

Books by Alistair Cockburn

Surviving Object Oriented Projects	1997
Writing Effective Use Cases	2000
Agile Software Development (1st ed)	2001
Patterns for Effective Use Cases	2002
People and Methodologies in Software Development (Dr. Philos. dissertation)	2003
Crystal Clear: A human-powered methodology for small teams	2004
Agile Software Development: The cooperative game (2nd ed)	2006
Design in Object Technology: Class of 1994	2021
Design in Object Technology: The Annotated Class of 1994	2022
Love Trio Trio del Amor (selected poems)	2022
Unifying User Stories, Use Cases, Story Maps	2024 2025
Hexagonal Architecture Explained.	2024 2025
Collaboration Cards: The Dance of Collaboration	2025
The Mini-Book on Use Cases	2025
Simplifying Software Design: The genius of bureaucracies, or how not-my-job sharpens your design	2026
The Book on Fine-Grained Incremental Development	2026

See the full list at https://alistaircockburn.com/Books